How to be Better at Managing People

How to be Better at Managing People

Alan Barker

KOGAN
PAGE

This one's for Sue

First published in 2000

Kogan Page Limited
120 Pentonville Road
London N1 9JN

© Alan Barker, 2000

British Library Cataloguing in Publication Data

A CIP record for this book is available from the British Library.

ISBN 0 7494 3196 2

Typeset by Kogan Page
Printed and bound in Great Britain by Clays Ltd, St Ives plc

CONTENTS

INTRODUCTION

Management is getting results through other people. It seems to me that poor managers – to hazard a grotesque generalization – fall into two groups: those who focus on results at the expense of people and those who care for people at the expense of results. Good management is being able to focus on both.

How you manage others will certainly determine your success as a manager. Yet this core function of management is regularly ignored, both by those who write on management and those who claim to be managers. This unwillingness may partly be because managing people is seen as so difficult – so full of ambiguity and complexity. Many people are promoted on the basis of their technical expertise. These able, committed experts then discover that management is not about applying technical expertise. Management resists easy technical explanations. It is not a job for a specialist, but for the opposite, a generalist. It requires a broad, generous outlook and a strong intuitive element.

The aim of this book is to help you manage those people for whom you have direct responsibility. As a manager, you have responsibilities to people in many directions (specifically five; we'll look at them later). This book is primarily about managing downwards, but many of us now manage projects, which adds a further complication to the task of managing people. I've ended the book, therefore, with a chapter on how to manage project teams.

I'm assuming you are not entirely new to the task of management. You are already in charge of one or more people. You're already doing it. You want to do it better. You're asking:

❑ What am I doing when I manage?

❏ Do I understand myself and others?
❏ How can I help people learn and develop?
❏ What creates good and bad work relationships?
❏ How do I influence my team?
❏ How do I handle conflict?
❏ What is communication without words?
❏ What makes meetings work?
❏ How can I influence my team's performance?
❏ How can I help people to manage change?
❏ What helps people to work better?

People are surprising. They are always capable of confounding our expectations, and they often do. People can't be labelled or defined. People are unpredictable. Above all, I believe that people *want* to do a good job. They *want* to make a contribution. Your task as their manager is to help them maximize that contribution.

I've planned the book as a sort of journey outwards. You want to start improving here and now. So I start with the most immediate tool of management: the conversation. I then place conversation within the most useful working model of management I know. Action-centred leadership is a picture of your responsibilities for managing people in three key areas: getting the work done, developing people as individuals and building your team. I devote one chapter to each of these broad areas. I end with a separate chapter on the special considerations of managing projects

I'd like this book to act as a gateway to other ways of learning and developing your skills. At the very end, I offer some suggestions for further development.

Throughout, I've used models to help you increase your understanding. Models simplify reality; good models simplify helpfully. In the thick of it, when life gets complicated, when people act unpredictably and when conversations get heated, we need models to help us see more clearly and act more rationally. The models in this book help me; I hope they will help you.

1

MANAGEMENT BY CONVERSATION

Let's start from where you are. You manage a number of people. They are 'your' people. They may or may not be organized as a team. You are responsible for them; they are answerable to you.

Management is getting results through other people. And the principal means by which you achieve that is conversation. Whatever systems or procedures you have in place, at the heart of your managerial role is conversation. Your ability to hold productive conversations will determine how well you:

❏ communicate objectives;
❏ gain commitment;
❏ resolve problems;
❏ review progress.

All managerial conversations seek a result. The result may be a clearer view of a problem, a choice between alternatives, a decision to take a particular course of action. It's in your conversations that you define what those results are, help your team to attain them and give feedback on their performance.

Management *is* a conversation. If you want to be better at managing people, the first place to start is with improving your managerial conversations.

COMMON MANAGERIAL PROBLEMS

Think about the most common results you need to achieve in managing people. There may be particular areas where you feel that you are challenged – specific managerial situations that you find difficult or would rather not have to face. Some of the most commonly quoted among managers include how to:

❑ manage conflict;
❑ convince people to do what I want;
❑ get people to do what they've agreed to do;
❑ negotiate more effectively;
❑ be firm without offending;
❑ persuade and influence;
❑ get people to cooperate;
❑ get people to solve problems more effectively;
❑ get people to think more creatively about their jobs;
❑ involve people more in planning their work.

All of these situations are managed through conversation.

WHY DO CONVERSATIONS GO WRONG?

We can all think of conversations at work that haven't turned out as we wanted. Working out why they went wrong is sometimes not simple. Conversations are so subtle and affected by so many factors. Few of us have been trained in the art of effective conversation. Conversation is a life skill, and – like most life skills – one we are usually expected to pick up as we go along.

Perhaps the key problem is that conversations are *fast*. It can be hard to analyse how we conduct a conversation as we hold it – let alone work out ways to improve it. One false move, made in the heat of the moment, can send a conversation into a fatal nosedive in a few seconds.

Let's reflect on some of the more general reasons why conversations fail. We might then be able to recognize some of them in the conversations we ourselves hold. Broadly, we might range these reasons under three headings:

❑ the context of the conversation;
❑ missing skills;
❑ mistaken assumptions.

The context of the conversation

Many conversations fail because the circumstances aren't right. For example:

❑ not enough time;
❑ the wrong time;
❑ an uncomfortable place;
❑ lack of privacy.

The problem may simply be that the conversation never happens. One of the most persistent complaints against managers is that they are not there to talk to. 'I never see him'; 'She has no idea what I do'; 'He simply refuses to listen'.

Missing skills

Every conversation includes certain moves, conventions and styles. We use them without thinking about them. Usually, they make conversations go more easily. If they are missing, the conversation can become limited and ineffective. Some of these missing skills include:

❑ starting the conversation without setting the scene;
❑ not listening;

❑ leaving things unsaid;
❑ saying things in code rather than directly;
❑ talking in terms of abstract ideas rather than specific details;
❑ dominating the conversation from one side;
❑ trying to develop ideas without enough facts;
❑ lack of summarizing;
❑ refusing to acknowledge what the other person is saying;
❑ closing without summing up or agreeing what to do next.

Mistaken assumptions

All conversations start from assumptions. If we leave them unquestioned, misunderstandings and conflict can quickly arise. For example, we might assume that:

❑ we both know what we are talking about;
❑ we need to agree;
❑ we know how the other person views the situation;
❑ we shouldn't let our feelings show;
❑ the other person is somehow to blame for the problem;
❑ we can be brutally honest;
❑ we need to solve the other person's problem;
❑ we're right and they're wrong.

Beneath these assumptions may lie deeper ones: mental models about the nature of the problem, about what kind of business we are in, about our role as a manager. The more we think about the models that underlie our conversations, the more seem to emerge!

Conversations often collapse into conflicts between such mental models. Instead of achieving a useful or productive outcome, we try to use our own mental model to beat the other person's into submission. This is *adversarial conversation*, and it is one of the most important reasons why conversations go wrong.

ADVERSARIAL CONVERSATION

Adversarial conversations set up a boxing match between competing mental models.

Any conversation is a dynamic of talking and listening. Most of us, however, are better at talking than at listening. At school, we are trained in the techniques of presenting, explaining and arguing for our ideas. We are taught the virtues of arguing: of taking a position, holding it, defending it, convincing others of its worth and attacking any position that threatens it.

In an attempt to impose some order on this conflict, we have invented debate (from the Latin, 'to beat down'). Much is made of the virtues of debate in management. Managers who can defend their ideas and withstand the onslaught of others gain status and may be promoted on the basis of their 'strong character'. They become company heroes and the stuff of myth. The implication is that debate is the best kind – perhaps the only worthwhile kind – of managerial conversation.

A debate is a conflict of rigid opinions. By the rules of debate, your opinions are somehow proved to be correct if you can successfully discredit any opposing opinions. You don't even have to prove that they are wrong; merely by ridiculing or discrediting the person voicing them you may be able to influence others to accept your opinion. As a means of reaching meaningful decisions, this is clearly a limited technique; yet debate is about the only formal structure of conversation that we know.

Opinions are ideas gone cold. They are our assumptions about what should be true, rather than conclusions about what is true in specific circumstances. Our opinions might include:

❑ stories (about what happened, what may have happened, why it happened);
❑ explanations (of why something went wrong, why we failed);
❑ justifications for doing what we did;
❑ gossip (perhaps to make us feel better at the expense of others);

❑ generalizations (to save us the bother of thinking);
❑ wrong-making (to establish power over the other person).

We often mistake opinions for the truth. Whenever you hear someone saying that something is 'a well-established fact', you can be certain that they are voicing an opinion.

The overwhelming problem with adversarial conversation is that it stops the truth from emerging. The clash and conflict of opinions actually prevents us from exploring and discovering ideas. And the quality of the conversation rapidly worsens: people are too busy defending themselves, too frightened, too battle-fatigued to do any better.

Adversarial conversations tend to develop four main kinds of thinking:

❑ critical thinking;
❑ ego thinking;
❑ rigid thinking;
❑ political thinking.

Look out for any of these in the conversations you hold. If you recognize one of them emerging, you can be certain that your conversation has become adversarial.

Critical thinking

For most of us, to think about anything is automatically to find what's wrong with it. Ask any of us what we think about something, and we are more likely to criticize it than to say why we like it.

The rationale behind critical thinking is that by looking for the weaknesses in an idea, we can strengthen it. But we rarely take criticism this way; instead we take it as criticism directed at us personally or as a rejection.

Ego thinking

In adversarial conversations, we rapidly become identified with our ideas. Reason becomes infected with emotion; debate is used as a pretext for point-scoring. We often find ourselves defending ideas that we may not feel strongly wedded to, because in defending the idea we are defending ourselves.

Rigid thinking

All conversations start with assumptions. Adversarial conversations merely strengthen the assumptions by pitting them against each other. The very form of the conversation forces us to make our assumptions more rigid. Rigid thinking is usually the result of:

❏ custom ('this is the way we do things around here');
❏ habit ('we've always done it this way');
❏ wilful ignorance ('thinking like this saves us the bother of trying to think another way').

Political thinking

When ideas become identified with people, the conversation becomes a way of forming alliances and destroying power bases. We begin to use conversational gambits, ploys and manoeuvres to play politics with ideas.

Adversarial conversations are self-perpetuating. They are cyclical and can easily escalate. Being attacked for our ideas causes pain; we respond in kind and help to prolong the conflict. We become locked into a 'cold war' of argument and counter-argument, of 'guerrilla tactics' and 'pre-emptive strikes'. We may feel that such conversations are unproductive and unpleasant, but we feel we cannot do anything different. We don't know how to, and we may be too frightened to try.

So, conversations can go wrong for a host of reasons: the wrong context, a lack of skills, unchallenged assumptions underlying what we say – above all, the tendency for managerial conversations to become adversarial. And if they go right, it may be more by good luck than good judgement. But managing people means being able to hold productive conversations with people that we might normally not hit it off with. We need to be able to *manage the conversation*.

WHAT IS A CONVERSATION?

A conversation is a means of creating shared understanding. This idea is well encapsulated in the increasingly fashionable word 'dialogue'. In dialogue, we construct a new, shared meaning *through* the conversation (the word is from the Greek, and means 'meaning through'). This is the ideal that all conversations should aim for: a shared understanding that comes into being as a result of holding the conversation.

Conversations are like verbal dances. The word 'conversation' derives from the Latin, 'to move around with'. Like any dance, a conversation has rules and standard moves. These allow people to move more harmoniously together, without stepping on each other's toes or getting out of step. Different kinds of conversation have different conventions. Some are implicitly understood; others – for example in presentations or meetings – must be spelt out in detail and rehearsed.

A conversation is a dynamic of talking and listening. We tend to think of conversations as people talking to each other; they are also people listening to each other. Without the listening, there's no conversation. These two activities don't merely happen in sequence; they occur simultaneously. Each participant in the conversation is both a speaker and a listener throughout the conversation.

The quality of the conversation depends more on the quality of the listening than on the quality of the speaking. Listening is the way we find out where the other person is standing, what they mean and how they think. Listening dictates how we move in the conversation. It's by listening that we find the common ground, the shared understanding we are looking for.

Listening is more than just not speaking, and more than hearing. The listener controls the speaker's behaviour by the way they listen: by maintaining eye contact, by their body position, by nodding or shaking their head, by taking notes and so on. Similarly, we demonstrate the quality of our listening to the other person whenever we speak. If we make a remark that the other person sees as irrelevant, they begin to doubt whether we have listened carefully. If we interrupt, we show that we don't want to listen. If we want to improve our conversations, a good place to start is with our listening skills.

BALANCING ADVOCACY AND ENQUIRY

Peter Senge, author of *The Fifth Discipline*, uses the words advocacy and enquiry to describe talking and listening. Talking is principally the means by which we advocate our point of view, our ideas, our thinking. Listening is the process of inquiring into the other person's point of view, their ideas, their thinking.

Adversarial conversations are pure advocacy. Each of us advocates our own point of view, reasonably and calmly, and we become more and more entrenched in our positions. Advocacy without enquiry simply escalates into conflict. You can see this escalation happening every day. It's exhausting and debilitating. It becomes part of the culture within which managers operate. It can be so upsetting that managers avoid holding conversations at all and retreat behind their office doors – if they are lucky enough to have them.

But conversations that are pure enquiry are also unsatisfactory. If we concentrate solely on listening to the other person, we risk an unclear outcome – or no outcome at all. Indeed, some managers use the skills of enquiry – listening, asking questions and always looking for the other point of view – as a way of avoiding difficult decisions.

The best conversations balance advocacy and enquiry. They are a rich mix of talking and listening, of stating views and asking questions.

IMPROVING YOUR LISTENING

We all know the symptoms of poor listening. They are so familiar that we come to expect them and even develop tactics for coping with them. They include:

❑ condemning an idea outright;
❑ criticizing the speaker's mode of delivery;
❑ only replying to a part of what the other person has said;
❑ interrupting;
❑ daydreaming;
❑ responding to a distraction;
❑ holding another conversation at the same time;
❑ evading the issue;
❑ using emotional language;
❑ going to sleep!

Conversely, we can all listen well when we are motivated to do so. For example, we may:

❑ like or admire the speaker;
❑ want to trip them up;
❑ think they have something interesting to say;
❑ expect to be rewarded for listening carefully;
❑ know that we will be asked to comment;
❑ have an overwhelming need to listen;
❑ know that effective listening makes us a better manager.

All conversations consist, for each participant, of *two* conversations: the external conversation and the internal conversation we hold inside our own heads. We must listen to both and take note of both. The danger is that the internal conversation will come to block out the external conversation.

Next time you hold a managerial conversation, listen to your internal conversation. What is it telling you? You may be:

❑ working out an answer;
❑ developing a solution;
❑ rehearsing your next remark;
❑ judging what the speaker is saying;
❑ concentrating on a part of what they have just said;
❑ comparing ideas to others in your mind;
❑ planning how to win;
❑ thinking up a quick getaway line;
❑ congratulating ourselves on being cleverer than the speaker;
❑ wondering about something completely different.

Some of these elements are clearly potentially helpful; others are not. Managing the inner conversation will help you to listen more actively to the external conversation: to listen to what the other person is saying, to what they are not saying, to the way they are saying it and the gaps in their remarks. Manage your inner conversation by:

❑ making notes of your 'inner' remarks so that you can put them to one side;
❑ vocalizing your internal conversation and bringing it into the external conversation;
❑ pausing before you speak, to listen to the internal conversation.

The ten commandments of effective listening

1. Stop talking. You can't listen if you are talking.

2. Demonstrate your interest. Maintain eye contact and allow the speaker to break their eye contact with you. Lean forward. Nod to indicate understanding. Ask questions. Take notes but don't doodle, shuffle, fiddle or look about.

3. Don't interrupt. Let pauses happen. Try not to finish sentences for the speaker.

4. Put yourself in the speaker's shoes. How might they feel about the situation, and about you?

5. Listen to your intuition. What might the speaker be saying with their eyes, their body, their gestures and posture? Test your intuition with careful questions.

6. Listen for triggers. Note down ideas you want to pick up later. Listen for colourful images and emotive language that you can explore and test.

7. Encourage. Avoid disagreeing or criticizing. Put the speaker at ease.

8. Check your understanding. Never assume that you know what the speaker means. Rephrase what they say in your own words.

9. Ask: 'What's good about the idea?' Accept and build on contributions to the conversation. Cultivate 'Yes and…' rather than 'No but…'.

10. Stop talking. This is the first and last commandment: all the others depend on it.

Using questions

Questions do more than any other kind of spoken contribution to improve the quality of the conversation. Use a full repertoire of questions to get the most information.

❏ **Closed questions** can only be answered 'yes' or 'no'. They are useful for establishing facts, for clarifying detail and removing ambiguity. They can also help to stop the conversation rambling.

❑ **Open questions** can't be answered 'yes' or 'no'. They serve to open up a conversation or focus on specific detail. They help you to establish ideas as well as facts. Open questions begin with one of the six words: *why, who, what, how, where* or *when*. It can be helpful to note down some open questions before holding a conversation.

❑ **Specific questions** seek particular details. They can pin a speaker down by demanding hard evidence for an idea.

❑ **Reverse questions** throw a remark, in a friendly way, back to the speaker. 'Do you mean...?', 'What do you think about what you've just said?'

The ladder of inference

Chris Argyris has developed a powerful model to help us use questions more effectively in conversations. Argyris pictures the way we think in conversations as a ladder. At the bottom of the ladder is observation; at the top, action.

❑ From our observation, we step onto the first rung of the ladder by selecting **data**. (We choose what to look at.)

❑ On the second rung, we infer **meaning** from our experience of similar data.

❑ On the third rung, we generalize those meanings into **assumptions**.

❑ On the fourth rung, we construct mental models (or **beliefs**) out of those assumptions.

❑ We act on the basis of our mental models.

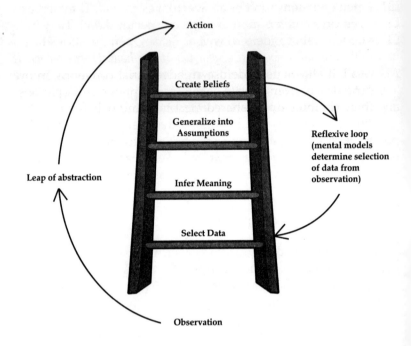

Figure 1.1 The ladder of inference

We travel up and down this ladder whenever we hold a conversation. We are much better at climbing up than stepping down. In fact, we can leap up all the rungs in a few seconds. These 'leaps of abstraction' allow us to act more quickly but they can also limit the course of the conversation. Even more worryingly, our mental models help us to select data from future observation, further limiting the range of the conversation. This is a 'reflexive loop'; you might call it a mind-set.

The ladder of inference gives us more choices about where to go in a conversation. It helps us to *slow down* our thinking, and allows us to:

❑ become more aware of our own thinking;
❑ make that thinking available to the other person;
❑ ask them about their thinking.

Above all, it allows us to defuse an adversarial conversation by 'climbing down' from private beliefs, assumptions and opinions and then 'climbing up' to shared meanings and beliefs.

The key to using the ladder of inference is to ask questions. The point is not to use it to score points but to find the differences in the way we think, what we have in common and how we might reach shared understanding. Here are some examples:

❑ 'What data underlie what you've said?'
❑ 'Do we agree on the data?'
❑ 'Do we agree on what they mean?'
❑ 'Can you take me through your reasoning?'
❑ 'When you say [what you've said], do you mean [my rewording of it]?'

If one person suggests a course of action, the other can carefully 'climb down' the ladder by asking:

❑ 'Why do you think this might work?', 'What makes this a good plan?'
❑ 'What assumptions do you think you might be making?', 'Have you considered...?'
❑ 'How would this affect...?', 'Does this mean that...?'
❑ 'Can you give me an example?', 'What led you to look at this in particular?'

Even more powerfully, the ladder of inference can help us offer our own thinking for the other person to examine. If we are suggesting a plan of action, we can ask them:

❑ 'Can you see any flaws in my thinking?'
❑ 'Would you look at this stuff differently?'

❏ 'How would you put this together?'
❏ 'Would this look different in different circumstances?'
❏ 'Are my assumptions valid?'
❏ 'Have I missed anything?'

The beauty of this model is that you need no special training to use it. Neither does the other participant in the conversation. You can use it immediately, as a practical way to intervene in conversations. It can become a powerful team tool, too. And it can have a powerful effect on the quality of your conversations as a people manager.

A MODEL FOR SKILFUL CONVERSATIONS

The ladder of inference gives you a useful model for intervening in your conversations to change their direction. It would be useful also to have a model for the overall *structure* of the conversations you need to hold as a manager. A simple framework will help you make your conversations more efficient and productive. It's important to remember that, as a manager, your conversations have two fundamental characteristics:

The conversation is objective-led
This is not simply a chat. You are holding the conversation for a reason. It should have an outcome. The outcome may not be what you thought it was going to be when you started the conversation.

You are in control of the conversation
You are the manager, and the conversation is taking place in the context of a managerial relationship. Of course, you may not have called the conversation. And controlling it doesn't mean that you dictate its progress or outcome. But it is up to you to take the lead in the conversation: to clarify that you understand why you are holding it, how you intend to conduct it, how long it will be and perhaps what you would like the outcome to be.

WASP: welcome – acquire – supply – part

In my early days as a manager I was introduced to a simple four-stage model of conversation that I have never forgotten. I still use it to help me keep my conversations in check and ensure that they have useful results. This is the **WASP** approach.

1. **Welcome.** In the first stage, you set the scene, bring yourself and the other person up to date, state your objectives and work out what you both know.
2. **Acquire.** The second stage, for you, is the listening stage. Here you concentrate on gaining knowledge from the other person rather than giving them information. The second stage of the conversation is characterized, for you, by questions: to find out more, to clarify, to put details into a bigger picture, to check that you understand what you have heard.
3. **Supply.** Now, at the third stage, you summarize what you have learnt and present the information you have to give. This includes information the other person may not know, as well as your interpretation of what they have told you. It's important at this stage of the conversation to remind yourselves of the objective that you set yourselves at the start.
4. **Part.** Finally, you work out what you have agreed. Above all, you state explicitly the outcome of the conversation: the action that will result from it. The essence of the parting stage is that you explicitly agree what is going to happen next. What is the action? Who will do it? Is there a deadline? Who is going to check on progress?

The WASP technique has been around for years. It's tried and tested. It works. It's simple and easy to remember. A key feature of the technique is that it encourages you to listen *before* you speak. This empowers the other person to give you the information that is important to them; it allows you to understand their point of view more clearly. This, in turn, gives you greater control of the conversation.

Virtually every intervention that we discuss in the rest of this book is based on this simple model. From impromptu conversations in the corridor to the most formal of interviews, WASP gives you a simple framework to make sure that the conversation stays on track and results in a practical outcome.

Four types of conversation

We can make this simple four-stage model more sophisticated. In this developed model, we hold four conversations, for:

❏ relationship;
❏ possibility;
❏ opportunity;
❏ action.

These four conversations may form part of a single, larger conversation; they may also take place separately, at different stages of a process or project.

A conversation for relationship
This is the 'welcome' conversation. Whatever you can accomplish with the people you manage is determined by your relationship with them. The terms of that relationship determine what you can say to each other and ask of each other; the boundaries of that relationship limit the actions you can commit to.

Think of your first meeting with somebody at a social event: the first few minutes are a clear example of a conversation for relationship. Managerial conversations for relationship go beyond social convention and finding common interests. They create the relationship you need to achieve your objectives. They set the terms of that relationship.

This conversation needs to happen at the start of any managerial relationship; it will probably need to be repeated as the terms of the relationship become blurred or get forgotten. Areas of responsibility and authority often need to be clarified on a task-by-task basis. So this is a conversation you will probably need to hold often.

A CONVERSATION FOR RELATIONSHIP: KEY QUESTIONS

- ❏ 'What are the bounds of our authority?'
- ❏ 'Where do we stand?'
- ❏ 'How do we relate to the matter in hand?'
- ❏ 'What links us?'
- ❏ 'How do we see things?'
- ❏ 'Where are the similarities and the differences?'
- ❏ 'Do you know things I don't know?'
- ❏ 'What do I know that you need to know?'
- ❏ 'How can we better understand each other?'
- ❏ 'Can we stand together on this?'

Conversations for relationship are sometimes tentative and awkward. As a result, we often rush them or pretend that they don't need to happen.

A conversation for possibility
This is the equivalent of the 'acquire' stage. A conversation for possibility is an exploration. It seeks to find new ways of looking at things, making distinctions without judging them. It's a conversation of questions.

A conversation for possibility is *not* about whether to do something, or what to do. It is about acquiring new information, as much as possible, and about generating ideas. It is a delicate conversation, partly because possibilities are always ambiguous and partly because we may both feel that the other person is judging us.

Because you are in control of the conversation, you must manage it with care. Make it clear that this is not decision time. Encourage the other person to give you ideas, and assure them that you won't hold them to account for any they offer. Take care not to judge or criticize. Do challenge or probe what the other person says. Use the ladder of inference. In particular, manage the emotional content of this conversation with care. This is the point where people's feelings are most likely to emerge in the conversation. Acknowledge those feelings and look for the evidence that supports them.

A CONVERSATION FOR POSSIBILITY: KEY QUESTIONS

- ❑ 'What's the problem?'
- ❑ 'What are we trying to do?'
- ❑ 'What's the real problem?'
- ❑ 'What are we really trying to do?'
- ❑ 'Is this a problem?'
- ❑ 'How could we look at this from a different angle?'
- ❑ 'Can we interpret this differently?'
- ❑ 'How could we do this?'
- ❑ 'What does it look like from another person's point of view?'
- ❑ 'What makes this different from last time?'
- ❑ 'Have we ever done anything like this before?'
- ❑ 'Can we make this simpler?'
- ❑ 'Can we look at this in bits?'
- ❑ 'What is this like?'
- ❑ 'What does this feel or look like?'

A conversation for opportunity
This corresponds to the 'supply' part of WASP. A conversation for opportunity is designed to map out what action you could take. It's fundamentally a conversation about planning. The bridge

from possibility to opportunity is *measurement*. In mapping out opportunities, you are interested in setting targets and identifying obstacles.

This is a conversation in which you supply more than acquire. After all, you probably know more about the opportunities for action than the person you are managing does. Hold this conversation to choose what to do. Assess what you need to achieve it: resources, time, support, skills. Range through the possibilities you have explored earlier and seek out those that are feasible. Take care here not to kill off possibilities by taking a limited view of opportunities. People are often far more capable of achieving goals than we imagine.

A CONVERSATION FOR OPPORTUNITY; KEY QUESTIONS:

- ❑ 'Where can we act?'
- ❑ 'What could we do?'
- ❑ 'Which possibilities do we build on?'
- ❑ 'Which possibilities are feasible?'
- ❑ 'What target do we set ourselves?'
- ❑ 'Where are the potential obstacles?'
- ❑ 'How will we know we've succeeded?'

Conversations for opportunity often collapse because we imagine the opportunities to be so limited. You can make them more imaginative and exciting by asking what the real objective is. Place yourself in a future where you have achieved your goal. What does it look like? What is happening? How are people acting? What do you need to do to achieve this future? Work backwards from there and identify the steps you need to take to get there. 'Backward planning' like this can often help you find new and simpler opportunities.

A conversation for action

The 'parting' conversation is a conversation for action. This is where you agree what to do, who will do it and when it will happen. Translating opportunity into action needs more than agreement; you need to generate a promise, a commitment to act.

Managers often remark that getting action is one of the hardest aspects of managing people. 'Have you noticed', one senior director said to me recently, 'how people seem never to do what they've agreed to do?' Following up on agreed actions can become a major time-waster. A conversation for action is the first step in pre-empting the problem. It's vital that the promise resulting from a conversation for action is recorded.

A CONVERSATION FOR ACTION: KEY STAGES

A conversation for action is a dynamic between asking and promising. It takes a specific form.

❑ You ask the other person to do something by a certain time. Make it clear that this is a request, not an order. Orders may get immediate results, but they rarely generate commitment.

❑ The other person has four possible answers to this request:
- they can accept;
- they can decline;
- they can commit to accepting or declining at a later date ('I'll let you know by...');
- they can make a counter-offer ('I can't do that, but I *can* do...').

❑ The conversation results in a promise ('I will do X for you by time Y').

This four-stage model of conversation, either in its simple WASP form, or in the more sophisticated form of relationship – possibility – opportunity – action, will serve you well in the wide range of encounters you must negotiate as a manager of people. Some of your conversations will include all four stages; some will concentrate on one more than another. But it's vital to remember that these conversations will only be truly effective if you hold them *in order*.

The success of each conversation depends on the success of the conversation before it. If you fail to resolve a conversation, it will continue underneath the next *in code*. Unresolved aspects of a conversation for relationship, for instance, can become conflicts of possibility, hidden agendas or 'personality clashes'. Possibilities left unexplored become lost opportunities. And promises to act that have no real commitment behind them will create managerial problems later.

2

MODELS OF PEOPLE MANAGEMENT

So far, we've seen that we manage people essentially through the conversations that we hold with them. We've seen how we can improve those conversations and give them structure.

Now we can step into a wider arena. Your conversations as a manager are based, at least in part, on your beliefs about your role as a manager. Those, in turn, will be affected by your underlying beliefs about what makes people tick. In this chapter, we'll examine some of those beliefs, and show how they probably relate to general models about the factors that motivate people at work.

Our aim is to develop a model that you can use to help you behave more consistently and rationally as a manager. Managing people is a complicated business; models help to simplify reality so that we can act more effectively.

What do you see as your overriding objective as a manager of people? Perhaps you would be happy when they do what you ask them to do, willingly and well. But the days of 'command and control', we are told, are over. Advances in technology, the increasing complexity of organizational structures and the wide range of new contractual arrangements that managers must operate within all mean that no single manager can be sure that they know what's best to do. Many people now work in matrix arrangements where they may have to answer to two or more managers (in project-based working, for example). Changes outside the workplace make people less and less willing simply to do what they're told.

In truth, most managers would want the people they manage to take more responsibility for their work. If the people we manage fully accepted the responsibilities that came with the job, and exercized them as mature adults, our work as managers would be easier.

Except... the more responsibility they take, the less knowledge and control we may have over them – and the more unmanageable they might become! This tension, between controlling people's action and giving them the freedom to behave responsibly, is at the very heart of people management.

WHAT'S YOUR MANAGEMENT STYLE?

Much has been written about 'management style'. From the 'autocratic manager' to the 'participative leader', just about every style of people management has its advocates and detractors. However much we may favour one style over another, the practical business of managing people means that we need to vary our style to suit the individuals and the circumstances.

Robert Tannenbaum and Warren Schmidt, in an important *Harvard Business Review* article in May 1973, identified seven broad styles of decision making in management, which they placed on a 'continuum of leadership behaviour'. We could think of these seven styles as seven types of conversation that you could hold with your team:

❑ **Tell**. At one end of the continuum, the manager makes the decision single-handed, with no attempt to involve others. This is effectively dictatorship.
❑ **Sell.** The manager makes the decision and tries to sell it to the team. Selling a proposal involves negotiating, identifying needs, promoting the benefits of the idea and being willing to accept the possibility of a 'failed sale'. Responsibility for the decision, though, remains with the manager.

❑ **Present.** The manager gives some of the background to the decision and invites questions so that the team can explore and understand it. Responsibility remains with the manager.

❑ **Suggest.** The manager suggests a possible course of action, invites discussion and review, but reserves the right to make the final decision.

❑ **Consult.** The manager consults the team in advance, making it clear that no decision has yet been made but that final responsibility remains with him or her. Others may offer their views and suggestions, and can be involved in the decision cycle. The manager promises to consider all views carefully, but still reserves the right to make the decision alone.

❑ **Ask.** At this point, the team takes responsibility for the decision. The manager defines the choice and the limits of the conversation.

❑ **Participate.** The team arrives at a joint decision with the manager's views carrying no more weight than anybody else's. The decision is made by consensus or by voting. The manager agrees to support the majority decision, even if not agreeing with it. They have effectively abdicated responsibility.

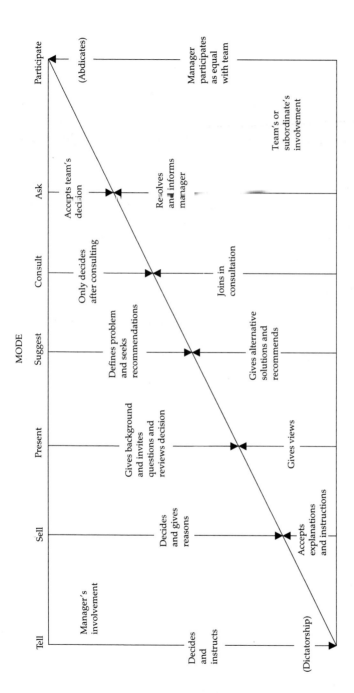

Figure 2.1 Conversations in management: seven styles

There is perhaps an increasing fashion to regard the 'telling' style of management as bad, and the 'participative' style as good. In reality, you will adopt different styles, depending on the type of decision you need to make. Telling may be the only credible option if the decision is urgent, critical, a matter of health and safety or entirely within your own sphere of responsibility.

THEORIES ABOUT PEOPLE AT WORK

Deep down, your choice of management style depends not only on circumstances but also on your beliefs about what drives people at work. Those beliefs are based primarily on your own experience – particularly your experience of being managed. If your first manager was an autocrat, for example, you may become an autocratic manager yourself. This cycle of autocratic management is common in organizations that are largely closed to outside influence, especially perhaps in certain professions. A writer examining the persistence of dictatorial managers among health professionals, for instance, has compared it to child abuse.

But you will also base your choice of managerial style on more widely held beliefs about what motivates people at work. These theories exist in society as a whole; they are what Richard Dawkins has called 'memes'.

Memes are ideas that pass from brain to brain, influencing our behaviour and transmitting what we normally call 'culture'. Memes aren't under our direct control; they enter our consciousness and determine the way we think about things. Strong memes become our own mental models; they can influence our behaviour as managers in subtle and far-reaching ways. In turn, our behaviour contributes to the strength of the meme in our society and makes it more influential.

Where do memes come from? Maybe behaviour and mental models are mutually reinforcing.

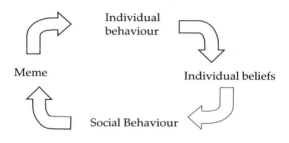

Figure 2.2 The meme cycle

The implication for managers is that, if we want to reinforce a mental model in the people we manage, we can do so by intervening in the cycle. Behave in ways that accord with a theory of human behaviour, and you will tend to strengthen that meme in other people. The key to changing people's ideas is *behaviour*.

A vast number of theories have emerged to explain what motivates people at work. Only a few have become powerful enough to count as memes. We'll look at some of them here.

McGregor's Theory X and Theory Y

Probably the most quoted of these mental models is based on Douglas McGregor's book, *The Human Side of Enterprise*, published in 1960. McGregor was a management consultant who drew up two sharply contrasting sets of assumptions about managing people.

Theory X– which McGregor saw as a typical or traditional view of employees by managers – assumes that people are lazy, dislike and shun work, and need both rewards and threats to do anything. Theory X assumes that most people can't take responsibility for themselves and need to be looked after. McGregor presumably developed Theory X from observation and interviews with managers.

Theory Y – which McGregor seems to have invented – posits the opposite. It assumes that people have a psychological need to work, achieve and take responsibility. Theory X assumes that people are mostly immature and that managers need to treat them rather as parents treat children. Theory Y assumes that people are – or want to be – mature adults.

This pair of theories has been hugely successful, probably for three main reasons:

❑ Theory X is easily recognizable as a widely-held belief among the general population (have you *never* felt that it held true for the people you manage?).
❑ Theory Y provides a clear, inspiring vision that managers can focus on easily.
❑ The pair of theories is simply presented and easy to remember.

There's no doubt that McGregor saw Theory Y as a model to help break the managerial stalemate of 'command and control'. Indeed, it has probably been one of the strongest influences in creating more human workplaces. And there's impressive evidence that Theory Y has some truth in it. Most of us, after all, want to work; most of us seek work that gives us satisfaction and a sense of achievement.

Theory X	Theory Y
People dislike work and will avoid it if possible.	Work is necessary to psychological growth.
People must be forced or bribed to put out the right effort.	People want to be interested in their work, and, under the right conditions, they can enjoy it.
People would rather be directed than accept responsibility.	People will direct themselves towards an accepted target. They will seek and accept responsibility under the right conditions. Self-discipline is more effective than any discipline imposed on them.
People are mainly motivated by money.	Under the right conditions, people are motivated by the desire to realize their own potential.
People are motivated by anxiety about their security. Most people lack creativity – except when getting round management.	Creativity and ingenuity are widely distributed and grossly underused.

Figure 2.3 McGregor's Theories X and Y

USING THEORY Y PRACTICALLY

Later research has shown that Theories X and Y are unsatisfactory as a theory of human nature. In fact, they are *memes*: mental models that influence behaviour.

The practical importance of Theory Y is not that it might be true, but that it tends to become true if you act *as if* you believe in it. If you, as a manager, act *as if* people are mature responsible adults, they will tend to behave as such. Theory Y gives us the beginnings of a strategy for people management.

Theory Y is a very attractive model of managerial behaviour. Why, then, is it sometimes so difficult to apply? The main reason is that we aren't all responsible adults. Or at least, not all the time. Abraham Maslow, a keen supporter of Theory Y, experimented with it when working with a small company in California. He concluded that Theory Y, attractive as it is, can be inhumane. For the weak, the vulnerable, the damaged, Theory Y demands too much. Even the strong and capable need a sense of direction, of security and order; the weaker among us need protection.

Maslow realized that Theory Y cannot simply replace Theory X. It's not simply a matter of removing 'command and control'; we must replace the security of Theory X with another kind of security. What commands and punishments do for Theory X must be achieved in some other way under Theory Y. If you want to use Theory Y as a strategy for managing people, you must realize that you risk making people feel lost and inadequate. Managing under Theory Y is not easier than under Theory X; it is far more difficult and complicated.

Maslow's hierarchy of needs

If we want the people we manage to behave like responsible adults, we need to satisfy the needs that prevent them from doing so. Maslow's own theory seeks to identify those needs. It predates McGregor's theory by two decades: Maslow first published his famous 'hierarchy of needs' in 1943. Although based on clinical observation of only a few neurotic individuals, this pyramid has achieved enormous influence as a general theory of human behaviour – particularly in management.

Maslow argued that human needs are ranked on five different levels. As a lower-order need is satisfied, it becomes less important, and needs on the next level gain in importance.

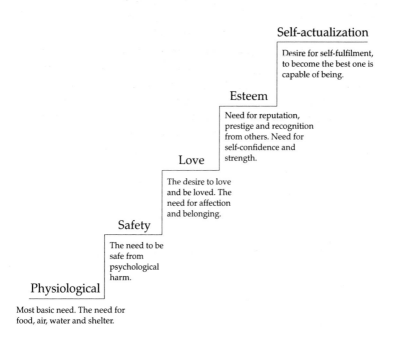

Figure 2.4 Maslow's hierarchy of needs

Maslow's theory has two important implications:

❑ Human needs emerge predictably, step by step. Once your physiological needs are satisfied – for food, shelter, warmth and so on – your need for safety becomes more prominent, and so on. Your need for 'self-actualization' cannot emerge until all the other needs have been met. For example, members of your team are unlikely to work responsibly if their need for respect and esteem remain unfulfilled.

❑ Needs are not absolute. The more a need is satisfied, the less interested we are in satisfying it. For example, if hunger is not a major need in your employees, you are unlikely to be able to motivate them to work harder by offering them more food.

It's interesting to note that Maslow's theory remains popular despite very little research evidence to either support or refute it. It seems to make sense that, if we want to help people to take more responsibility, we must satisfy their needs for security on the lower levels of Maslow's hierarchy.

On the other hand, it's possible to think of situations where people are motivated to great acts of self-actualization despite, or with no care for, satisfying their lower-level needs. Creative people, for example, may take little interest in satisfying their physiological needs. Graded pay scales, comfortable furniture and a well-stocked canteen may make little difference to their motivation. On the other hand, they may demand a great deal of freedom to express and fulfil themselves in their work.

What Maslow perhaps did not realize is that a need changes in the act of being satisfied. For example, if people become accustomed to having their basic needs met – through regular pay, for example – it may become less of an incentive but far more powerful as a source of *dis*satisfaction if it is suddenly removed or reduced. A need can also change by becoming a different kind of need. To take the example of pay once more: when everybody is paid enough to buy what they need to survive, pay itself becomes a factor in satisfying people's need for esteem. A great deal of dissatisfaction can arise from a relatively small difference in pay scales.

USING MASLOW'S HIERARCHY OF NEEDS PRACTICALLY

Maslow remains a powerful model for many managers. It gives you a set of indicators to check against the behaviour of your team.

❑ Use Maslow to get the basics right. Your team is unlikely to perform at its peak if the fundamental issues of comfort, safety and respect for individuals are unresolved.
❑ Use Maslow to identify your team's most powerful current need. You can also use it as a tool to help you set targets that seek to satisfy higher-level needs.
❑ Use Maslow to identify blockages in people's development. If your team is working under threats to their lower-level needs – redundancy, relocation, danger or discomfort – you may find it more difficult to develop their achievements at higher levels. This is more likely to be true perhaps if the lower-level threats are new.

Locke's theory of goal-setting

Theories based on psychological models have proved highly influential but difficult to support in terms of actual performance. By contrast, goal-setting has consistently been proved to achieve higher results than any other motivational technique – and yet it remains relatively unexplored and unknown among managers generally.

Highly motivated people certainly tend to be goal-oriented. 'If you don't know where you're going', the Cheshire Cat tells Alice, 'any road will take you there.' As a manager, you are in a position to set and agree goals with the people you manage. They are perhaps the most powerful tools you can wield to motivate them to higher and more focused performance.

Goals have long been recognized as a major factor in motivating people to perform at work. Indeed, in recent years a whole management philosophy – management by objectives – has grown up around goal-setting.

Edwin Locke has developed one of the clearest models of goal-setting. Locke conducted hundreds of studies investigating the effect of goal-setting on performance.

Locke concludes that goals motivate people in four main ways:

❑ **Goals direct our attention**. If we are committed to achieving a goal, we are more likely to focus our attention on what we need to think and do to achieve it. A less kind way of putting this might be: 'What gets measured gets done.'

❑ **Goals regulate our efforts.** A goal is likely to increase the amount of work we put into achieving something than a general hope or wish.

❑ **Goals make us more persistent.** Persistence is effort over time. We are more likely to persist at a goal to which we are committed.

❑ **Goals help us plan.** If you are here and the goal is to be there, you are encouraged to develop a structured plan to make the journey. You are more likely to plan a weight-loss programme, for example, if you give yourself a realistic goal than if you simply decide to lose weight.

Reviews of goal-setting over the decades since 1968, when Locke first proposed his ideas, have led to five main insights about goal-setting that managers can find useful:

❑ **Difficult goals lead to higher performance**. Goal difficulty relates to the amount of effort required to achieve the goal. It's more difficult to swim 100 metres in 30 seconds than in 50 seconds. It's more difficult to sell 10 washing machines a month than only 1. Difficulty, remember, is *perceived* difficulty. Goals that are perceived to be impossible lead people to perform more poorly.

❑ **Specific goals lead to higher performance than general or 'do your best' goals.** This result is generally only true for simple goals. People will not perform complicated tasks well, no matter how specific the goal, unless they have a clear strategy for achieving them.

❑ **Feedback enhances performance.** Feedback is essential to many activities. Imagine trying to play darts if you cannot see the dartboard. Yet many people have to perform tasks at work with little or no feedback from their managers. Feedback lets people know if they are on course.

❑ **Goals can be self-set, assigned or agreed.** Clearly, someone is more likely to be committed to a goal they have at least participated in setting. But there is no clear evidence that any one way of setting goals is better than another.

❑ **People will only achieve goals if they are committed to them.** This is the most crucial element. At this point, the argument for goals as motivators becomes circular. In certain circumstances, it's clear that setting the goal itself *creates* the commitment to achieve it (the 'rah-rah' effect). It remains unclear whether monetary or other kinds of reward are effective in gaining commitment to goals.

Goals or targets are now more than ever an organizational norm. It's very likely that you are working in a culture where goals are common, or being introduced – perhaps against resistance. We shall examine goal-setting in more detail in the next chapter. For the moment, it's important to emphasize that goals – properly set and carefully monitored – will probably help you manage people according to Theory Y. Goals can provide a realistic substitute for Theory X's commands and sanctions. They deliver a key element of security: they give people a clear sense of where they belong, where they are going and what they need to achieve. Goals are an essential part of helping the people you manage to take more responsibility.

USING GOAL-SETTING PRACTICALLY

There are three steps to take in setting goals:

❑ **Set specific goals**. Make them measurable.
❑ **Promote goal commitment.** Involve people as much as possible in setting goals. Explain why you believe in them and why the organization is setting them. Present the corporate goals and explain how individual goals fit in. Encourage people to set their own goals and always push for difficult, but not impossible, goals. Train yourself and your team in goal-setting.
❑ **Provide feedback.** Motivation without knowledge is useless. Unless people know how well they are doing, and what is expected of them, they cannot judge and adjust their own performance. Feedback also helps people to develop their skills.

ACTION-CENTRED LEADERSHIP

Both McGregor's theories and Maslow's hierarchy of needs develop a psychological attitude to human behaviour. Even Locke's goal-setting theory assumes that people will behave as they do for psychological reasons. As managers, we do indeed need to know more about human beings. It's surely better to think about people as people, rather than cogs in some corporate machine.

But managers aren't paid to be psychologists (except, perhaps, heads of psychology departments!). We are not paid to look after people, to attend to their every need, to heal and comfort. We are paid to get results. A doctor looks after a patient's health; a manager must look to the needs of the task they are paid to achieve. Our focus in managing people must be on the job. The job is not everything; but it does come first.

So your effectiveness as a manager depends on your ability to influence others – and to be influenced by them – to achieve a task. In practice, this means that the people you manage need to know:

❑ what the task is;
❑ how they are doing;
❑ where they belong.

Your responsibility is to:

❑ achieve the task;
❑ develop the skills of individuals;
❑ build the team.

A successful manager pays attention to all three areas of responsibility. Three interlocking circles can represent this model of responsibility: the famous three circles of John Adair's concept of action-centred leadership. The circles interlock because neglecting one area has inevitable consequences in the others.

Lack of attention to the task, for example, causes demoralization in the team and dissatisfaction in the individual. By the same token, concentrating too much on one area may cause the others to become neglected. A manager who is too task-oriented may fail to develop people adequately; a strong preference for developing individuals or the team may mean that tasks are neglected.

Achieving the task

The job comes first. Accomplishing the various tasks for which your role and your team exist is your most obvious duty. The danger – especially if you are pursuing goals or targets – is that you will try to do it all yourself. It may be that you can do the job better than your team; but that's not your job. Your responsibility as a manager is to achieve tasks *through* the people you manage. For a manager, achieving the task means:

❑ being clear what the task is, communicating it to your team and reminding them of it often;
❑ understanding how tasks fit into the overall plans of the organization;
❑ planning how to accomplish the task;
❑ providing the necessary resources: people, time, money, equipment, authority;
❑ doing whatever you can to ensure that the organizational structure allows people to accomplish the tasks;
❑ providing feedback on progress;
❑ evaluating results in the light of plans and objectives.

Figure 2.5 Action-centered leadership (after John Adair)

Developing individuals

Your team is made up of individual human beings. People aren't machines and don't work like machines. We have needs – Maslow has taught us this – before, during and after the work we do. We need to live and express ourselves as individuals, to provide for ourselves, our partners or families, to find satisfaction in what we do, to win acceptance and respect from our peers. Perhaps most importantly, we need to feel that we are making a contribution.

Fortunately for you, the manager, all of these needs mean that people *want* to be involved in their work and do it well. They *want* to be motivated.

*Un*fortunately, too much work is still organized as if people were mechanical. (Stress at work is largely the result of treating people like machines.) Machines work best when they do only one, simple task, repeatedly. They work best if run at a constant speed and rhythm, with a minimum of moving parts. People, by contrast, are not suited to repetitive, single operations. We lack strength and stamina. We tire easily. We make mistakes. What we *are* good at is coordination. We work best when the entire person – mind, senses, muscles – is involved in the work.

So the best kind of work for people is work that consists of groups of operations. If we can switch our attention fairly often from one task to another, we will work more efficiently. If we can understand how the tasks fit meaningfully together, we will work more effectively. If we can vary both the speed and the rhythm of our work frequently, so much the better. And if we have *control* over these variations of speed and rhythm, better still.

Developing the mental and physical skills of people at work, then, is an absolute necessity if we want them to work as well as possible. You have a core responsibility as a manager to help people feel that:

❑ they are getting personal satisfaction from their work;
❑ they are making a worthwhile contribution to their team and their organization;

❑ they find their work challenging;
❑ they have a degree of responsibility that they can handle comfortably;
❑ their contribution is recognized (and, perhaps, rewarded);
❑ they have genuine control over those aspects of their work for which they are responsible;
❑ their work is helping them to develop and grow in experience, ability and maturity.

This aspect of management is perhaps the most neglected. Too often, senior management proclaims that 'people are our greatest asset' while doing little to invest in them. There is a real danger, too, that this aspect of your role as a manager can fall by the wayside in the pursuit of 'getting things done'. Developing individuals is an aspect of your work that you simply cannot afford to ignore. If you do, people will vote with their feet.

Building the team

Most of us work in teams. Teams have their own identity, their own histories and their own patterns of growth and decay. No two teams are alike. The key insight for a team manager is that teams have needs *different* from those of the individuals in them. So you need to be able to respond to the dynamics of the team you lead and to represent them in the wider organization. Building the team means:

❑ setting and maintaining team objectives;
❑ establishing and promoting team values: social, behavioural, task-oriented;
❑ maintaining the identity of the team;
❑ helping the team always to be outward-looking: welcoming new people and ideas, being proactive in the wider organization and with customers or partners;

❑ communicating effectively with the team and helping team members communicate with each other;
❑ involving the team as much as you can in decisions that relate to them.

Management is not a theory but a practice. What matters is not what you know but what you do. This is why the working model we've looked at in this chapter is called 'action-centred leadership'. Your focus as a manager must be on *action*.

Action-centred leadership takes us beyond questions of managerial style (such as Tannenbaum and Schmidt's continuum). Managing people is a living process that is continually shifting its emphasis between task, individuals and team. The management style we adopt will depend critically on which area of responsibility we are addressing at the time.

The crucial question is not 'What sort of manager do I want to be?' but 'What is the reality of my situation and how can I make my contribution as a manager in this situation?' The theories and models we have examined here are useful in helping us to understand the reality of our situation; but the quality of our management will be tested in practice.

MANAGING YOURSELF

You cannot manage other people if you cannot first manage yourself. Often, problems in the way people are managed can be traced to inadequate self-management on the part of the manager. Good managers lead by example. If you are unwilling to manage your own contribution – in achieving your own tasks, in developing yourself, in contributing as an effective team member – then you have no right to expect others to behave any better.

This chapter, then, is about knowing yourself and your role. We shall look at how you can apply action-centred leadership to yourself, and how you might overcome some of the tensions implicit in your position as a manager: tensions that, left unresolved, may damage your performance.

FIVE-WAY MANAGEMENT

Every modern manager has responsibilities in five directions:

❑ **Managing downwards.** You are entrusted with certain resources, of which the most valuable is people. The people who report directly to you, whom you appraise, are your primary responsibility in managing downwards.

❑ **Managing upwards.** You may have no choice about who your manager is, but your relationship with that person will make all the difference to your own performance and job satisfaction. Managing upwards means understanding your manager's job and recognizing the value of their contribution to the organization. It also means trying to develop more powerful and honest conversations with them. In some organizations, 360-degree appraisal is an attempt to help people manage their managers more effectively.

❑ **Managing across the organization.** As a manager, you will deal with other managers in other departments, or teams, or areas, or even regions. Your relationships with them as individuals will affect how all of you perform. Problems arise particularly when managers of specialist functions must hold conversations to achieve common objectives. Marketing and Production speak different languages; Operations and Finance may not be on speaking terms at all. Service level agreements between departments may set down some basic ground rules about how we communicate across the functional boundaries. Finally, however, it's down to you to make the effort to understand each other to the extent necessary to achieve your objectives. And as project management takes hold, the need to manage effectively across those boundaries becomes urgent.

❑ **Managing outwards.** The range of your contacts outside the organization is probably much larger than you think. It will include customers, suppliers and business partners, of course; but it may also include regulators, inspectors, solicitors, researchers, the media, schools, professional bodies... With some of these contacts you will have complete freedom of management; with others, only a little; and with a third group – auditors, regulators, inspectors and assessors – virtually none at all. You will need to find ways of managing them all.

❑ **Managing yourself.** You are at the centre of it all. The way you manage yourself will determine how you manage all of your other managerial relationships.

The five-dimensional management model is a useful self-auditing tool. By examining your strengths and weaknesses in each dimension, you can build up a strategy for improving your skills. All of which will help you to manage yourself even better.

DEFINING YOUR CONTRIBUTION

You should be striving to build effective relationships upwards, downwards, outwards and across the organization. But an equal priority is to manage yourself, to 'get your own act together'.

So your first opportunity to use five-way management is to take stock of your personal contribution to the organization. Start this analysis yourself, and then talk it through with a colleague. The analysis is in two parts:

❑ looking at the job itself;
❑ looking at your personal contribution to it.

Think first about the reason for the job. If you are the customer service manager, why does that role exist? Or if you are a quality coordinator, why was the role created?

THINKING ABOUT THE JOB

Questions to ask yourself include:

❑ What is the special contribution of this role?
❑ What makes it different from other similar posts?
❑ How up-to-date is the job description?
❑ Does the job title accurately reflect the job's demands?
❑ Is the reality of the work significantly different from what it is supposed to be?
❑ How well understood is this job in the organization?

You may find it helpful to discuss your responses to these questions with a colleague. It can be difficult to disentangle the job from yourself as the jobholder.

The second stage of this analysis is to look at your personal contribution. You may have created the role from scratch, or inherited it from a not-very-competent predecessor, or taken over from a much respected manager. Whichever route brought you into the role, you will have made it your own in all sorts of ways. What is the 'added value' that you bring?

THINKING ABOUT YOUR CONTRIBUTION

Questions that may help you are:

- ❑ What changes did I make when I took on this job?
- ❑ Which aspects of the job consume most of my time?
- ❑ What do I find most difficult in the job?
- ❑ What do I find enjoyable about the work?
- ❑ What do I find frustrating?
- ❑ Does the role use all of my skills? If not, which are getting rusty?
- ❑ How good are my relationships with colleagues, my team, my manager, and external contacts?
- ❑ What one piece of advice will I give to my successor when the time comes?

Once you have gone through this analysis, first of your job then of your personal contribution, you can use five-way management to consider whether there is a good match between the job and your own contribution.

Managing upwards

Are you encroaching on your manager's role? Perhaps you are nib-bling at responsibilities that are rightfully theirs. If you are, it's not necessarily anything to be ashamed of. Perhaps you're ready for more responsibility, in which case you can open up that dialogue.

Managing downwards

Are you second-guessing what your team are doing? Are you breathing down their necks? Are you giving them enough scope to let them do things their way? It may not be your way, but it might be equally effective.

Managing outwards

How much does 'firefighting' take up your time? Are you taking a proactive stance, using your antennae to predict customers' requirements or regulators' demands? Or are you always on the defensive, reacting to external influences?

Managing across the organization

Is there overlap between yourself and any colleagues? Have you agreed mutual boundaries or do you carry out border raids on your colleagues' areas? The actual boundaries of your role (up, down outwards and across) are probably fluid; you may have made them that way. This is not necessarily wrong. It may simply reflect reality: you have moulded the job to fit your skills.

You need to take a realistic and flexible approach to role defini-tion. Of course the organization needs to achieve its objectives – and so do you – but the days are surely past when your job responsibilities need to imprison you in a rigidly defined job description. Indeed, few managers could survive without a more open attitude to their work. The danger, of course, is that such fluidity leads to overwork: an ever more common problem in organizations that have 'downsized'. Better to negotiate with those whose roles are adjacent to your own, and adjust the boundaries so that everybody has a chance of winning – or at least surviving.

But there are two other checks you need to make on the actual shape of your role:

❑ **Look for black holes.** Are there any responsibilities that you are uncomfortable with and dislike, so that either they are never achieved or else they are tackled half-heartedly? We all have something of this kind: mine is budgeting. I am glad to delegate it rather than carry it out myself, but I remain accountable for fulfilling my budget commitments – they cannot be delegated.

❑ **Look for unused skills.** What skills do you have that your role does not require? For example, you may be able to speak Spanish but the job description says nothing about foreign languages.

YOUR OWN DEVELOPMENT

Your own development matters just as much as that of the people you manage. You may be able to explore the possibilities for your own development with your manager, through appraisal and linked development plans such as those in this book. Increasingly, managers are given the opportunity – or sometimes given the one option – of pursuing self-development. You may come across the idea as self-managed learning for self-directed development. Self-managed learning means using the range of learning resources and opportunities available to you according to a plan that you control. But no self-respecting organization should let you attempt this plan alone. You must work to recognize your needs, make them explicit, create a support network and review your own progress. Your organization, for its part, should offer you opportunities to train and learn, foster a climate of learning and a network of learning support, and provide you with work opportunities to use the new skills, knowledge and attitudes that you develop.

You probably have some skills that you don't use at work. You owe it to yourself and to your employer to make these skills known, and see if they can be put to use within the work situation. After all, they are what we are good at and enjoy, so why not deploy them?

Identifying and exploiting your own unique blend of skills is the best contribution you can offer your organization. For example, if you are one of a team of design engineers but you happen to be brilliant at chairing meetings, your company may well benefit most if you spend three-quarters of your time chairing meetings (on any subject) and simply 'keep your hand in' with some design work.

MAKING TIME TO MANAGE

If you have gone to all the trouble of identifying your own contribution, it stands to reason that you should aim to operate at your added value level for as much of the working week as possible. As a manager, your time should be taken up mostly with that very activity: managing others. All too often, though, you can find yourself engaged in activity that is *not* management, leaving you with all too little time to devote to your primary role.

Three tough time questions

If you begin to hear rumours that your team never see you and never get the chance to talk to you, you need to ask some tough questions about the way you manage your time:

❑ What am I doing that doesn't need to be done?
❑ What am I doing that someone else can do?
❑ What am I doing that wastes other people's time?

The first question throws up issues of priorities and meaningless paper shuffling. The goal here must be to separate what's important from what's merely urgent. Set your goals and ask yourself each day what you propose to do to achieve them. Make your plans and keep to them. For everything else, you need a system.

THE SYSTEM FOR 'EVERYTHING ELSE'

❑ **Clear your workspace**. It really is true that a tidy desk makes for tidy use of time.
❑ **Get the tools to do the job.** Diary, wallchart, bring-forward file, daily action list. I use shorthand notebooks to record daily actions, occasional phone numbers and so on. I keep them all in a cupboard: all my daily rough notes from the first day I took the job.
❑ **Handle each piece of paper once only**. Clichéd advice, but it works.
❑ **Plan your use of phone and e-mail.** You need to be available to take calls. Make a time and tell people when you will be there. You may be able to make calls in batches. Catch your e-mails twice a day – no peeping at other times!

The second question encourages you to think about delegation. We discuss this important issue in Chapter 5. The last question, perhaps, requires the greatest effort of will. Call it self-indulgent dabbling in other people's business.

How often do you pick up the phone to talk to someone who doesn't *need* to hear from you at that moment? How often do you find yourself wandering the office in search of stimulating conversation (perhaps under the disguise of 'walking the job'!)? How often do you send your colleagues information that they have no use for, and will never read?

Self-indulgent dabbling may mean that you are dipping in and out of the part of your role that you most enjoy, but that isn't the most productive. For example, I sometimes fall into the habit – under the disguise of 'research' – of scanning the newspapers for interesting stories, which I carefully cut out and inflict on my colleagues. I think, deep down, I see it as my role to keep them up-to-date – to educate them a bit. Vastly enjoyable – but maybe not the most productive way to spend the first hour of the morning.

A more damaging type of self-indulgent dabbling is where you cannot quite let go of the previous post you held, and you continue to meddle in it. If this post is in someone else's department, your meddling will not be tolerated for long. But if you have been promoted from within your own team, you may be looking over the shoulder of your successor in that role and restricting their headroom. The best cure is to apply the added-value principle. For you to operate at your added-value level, you must allow everyone else to operate at theirs.

Managing your time five-ways

You can use five-way management to make regular checks on how you divide your time between the five areas. This does not mean exactly 20 per cent on each; it means being proactive, making sure that the proportions are as you wish them to be. For instance, many managers acknowledge that they should indeed be with their team more, but are forever closeted in meetings at a 'higher' level.

Five-way management provides a route to alter the proportions the way you wish. The 'managing yourself' area acts rather like a junction box.

Suppose you are bogged down by internal meetings and want to get away from the office to visit suppliers. Rather than make New Year resolutions about it that collapse by mid-March, set yourself a measurable change, perhaps to cut half a day a week from meetings (managing across) and transfer that time to supplier visits (managing outwards).

To achieve this switch, your route takes you through 'managing yourself', where you ask 'How can I do that?' Some of the time could be saved by you only attending a particular part of a meeting rather than sitting through the whole agenda: you could ask a colleague (managing across) to brief you on any remaining items you need to know about. The rest of the time is produced by delegating another meeting to one of your team (managing downwards).

The 'managing yourself' junction box can also enable you to distinguish between urgent and important. Suppose you realize that you are spending too much time away from your team, firefighting problems (urgent). Your team is suffering because you haven't found time to work out a strategy with them (important) – which is one of the reasons why so much firefighting is called for. You need to shift some priority from managing outwards to downwards. For one month, you give a colleague (managing across) the authority to handle the 'outwards' urgent issues without referring back to you. During that month you work with your team to create the clear strategy.

Redistributing your time through five-way management is not rocket science. But managers who consciously use the five-way approach report that it strengthens their determination to make time management work. As one manager said to me, 'It puts you in the driving seat.'

DEALING WITH STRESS

Many recent surveys have concurred that stress levels at work are alarmingly high. The results are absenteeism, insularity and a damaging lack of creativity. As managers, we have a dual responsibility:

to keep our own stress at a reasonable level and to avoid inflicting stress on others.

Five-way management provides a good framework to identify the sources of stress (from our immediate manager; from our direct reports; from colleagues; from external organizations) and how we might be unwittingly inflicting stress on others.

The difficulty is that, by definition, we experience stress as something that happens to us. We always see the source of stress outside us. Occasional stress may be positively helpful. Deadlines can stimulate creativity. (I would prefer to see this as creative tension rather than imposed stress.) Some people operate at their very best under pressure, perhaps because it allows them to 'manufacture' a sense of external crisis that they can then overcome in heroic fashion. And certainly a short adrenaline rush can be pleasurable.

When stress is prolonged, however, it does great harm. And you are being selfish if you overlook the impact on others of your own sense of stress. Your irritability, abruptness and short temper affects others no less than yourself.

There are five actions you can take to keep your own stress within civilized bounds:

❑ **Do what's important.** If you allow yourself to be diverted by trivial issues, and to procrastinate ('I'll put off writing that big report for another week'), you're only fooling yourself and storing up trouble. Great job satisfaction comes from looking back over a week's work and knowing that for much of the time you were delivering what you were uniquely placed to deliver, to the organization and to your team. Delegate. Learn to say 'No'.

❑ **Manage outwards to change your perspective.** We all have times when nothing seems to go right, and it is easy to become sucked into a vicious spiral. You can even start to feel a little paranoid, as if everything is conspiring against you. When this happens, try very hard to make some space in your diary to get away from your normal workplace for a day. Go and visit another branch, or a customer or supplier, or accompany a colleague on their travels. This should help to give you a sense of perspective.

❑ **Ask for help.** The natural ups and downs of working life create problems for everyone sooner or later. It is simply common sense to recognize this. Asking for help from colleagues is *not* a sign of weakness. We can all help each other in all sorts of ways: borrowing a member of another team to overcome a peak of work, or negotiating a little extra time on a deadline.

❑ **Let off steam.** Build in 'downtime'. You need it: you are not a machine. (Even machines need downtime!) Schedule this to suit your natural rhythms. It may be better to push yourself in the mornings and relax a little in the afternoons. What you do in this time is very much a matter of individual preference. Physical exercise certainly has mental benefits. I know that I can think better after 20 lengths in the swimming pool.

❑ **Find out the 'why' behind the 'what'.** Develop your understanding of the work you are doing. Strive to comprehend the context, the bigger picture. Build your skills to allow you to take more command of your situation. Don't take requests or demands at face value. If I ask you to do something, I stand a much better chance of gaining your wholehearted commitment to it if I give you the reason behind the request. 'I need this by Tuesday because...'; 'We have to redraft this in order to...'. So if your manager, or a colleague, or an inspector, makes a request that seems opaque or unreasonable, ask for the background. If you know why, you and your team will be better placed to fulfil the request effectively.

4

MANAGING THE WORK

Managing other people's work is essentially a matter of setting a contract. Each side contributes to an agreement about what the work is, where the limits of authority and responsibility lie, and how performance is going to be measured.

We all need to know what our roles and responsibilities are. At the heart of this contract between the manager and the person managed is the idea of *action responsibility*. This concept is that each person is uniquely responsible for what they do themselves, and *not* responsible in the same way for what other people do.

Your action responsibility defines your true power. It sets out the extent to which you can make things happen. Within the space of your action responsibility, you exercise authority and autonomy; others may not encroach upon that space without your permission.

DEFINING THE JOB

Defining someone's action responsibilities is a difficult but worthwhile exercise. You might start by sitting down with the person you manage and briefly discussing your own job. Ask them what they know about your own action responsibilities, and fill in the gaps. Sharing information like this is good preparation for tackling their job.

You might move on immediately, or suggest that they consider privately their own work in the same way and bring back some notes. At this second stage, ask the question: 'What do you do at work?' The answers must be honest and accurate. They should be specific and expressed using strong verbs. The fudging words of the traditional job description – to ensure this, to control that, to manage something else – are inadequate. What do you do to ensure, control or manage? Aim for strong, specific answers.

It's a daunting prospect. You might begin by mapping out three main areas of responsibility within which the person works:

❑ technical responsibility;
❑ administrative responsibility;
❑ personnel responsibility.

You might then develop these areas in more detail. You might already have structures in place to define these areas of responsibility: they might be called *key result areas, key measures* or *key values*. It is important not to let terminology get in the way here; different organizations inevitably use different words to express the same idea.

Key result areas

Key result areas are the broad areas where we discharge our action responsibilities. They are also the areas within which we can define goals or targets. The names of key result areas for any particular job will be determined by its overall objective – the reason it exists – and the broader activities of the organization. You shouldn't need to use more than about four to six.

KEY RESULT AREAS: COMPARISONS

Here are some key result areas used by different organizations:

❑ **quality, output, costs, time, staff, customers** (food manufacturer);
❑ **shareholder value, product quality, people quality, customer satisfaction** (automotive manufacturer);
❑ **quality, costs, deadlines, punctuality, customer service, safety** (bus company);
❑ **leadership and the individual, quality, customer service, partnerships, team working** (housing association).

Of course, the words defining the key result areas may themselves differ from organization to organization. The important thing is that you and the jobholder both understand clearly what they mean.

Now set out the specific responsibilities that the person must discharge within each area. Discuss any points where your view of the job differs from theirs. You will probably feel that they have exaggerated some actions and underestimated others; they will undoubtedly feel – with good reason – that they understand the job better than you can. The conversation is aiming at agreement: a shared perception of the person's action responsibilities, their order of priority and the way in which they should be discharged.

Performance standards

Once you have established what the jobholder's action responsibilities are, you need to agree how to judge whether their performance is acceptable. Performance standards set the levels at which you both consider that the work is happening at an acceptable level. Don't confuse these with *targets*, which are specific

---

goals to aim for. Targets relate to an individual and tend to be short-term; performance standards relate to the job and are more long-term.

If you don't set performance standards, the jobholder will find it difficult to know what's expected of them or how they are doing. Both of you need to agree what those standards are.

SETTING STANDARDS

You can set standards in six areas:

- ❑ **numeric:** sales or production figures, defect levels, paper flow, visitor rates;
- ❑ **deadlines:** project completion, turnaround of correspondence, statutory time limits, regular meeting dates, time taken to answer the phone;
- ❑ **financial:** working to budget, meeting profit forecasts, stock levels, cost reduction;
- ❑ **procedural:** stages in completing a project, liaison systems, time spent on regular operations;
- ❑ **negative:** numbers of complaints, feedback from colleagues, cancellations;
- ❑ **recognizable:** corporate approach to customers, standards of dress, presentations to meetings, house style.

Performance standards must be objective. In other words, you should be able to measure or at least recognize them. They should cover quality as well as quantity. Creating quality performance standards is notoriously difficult. It's easy to measure the number of calls a helpline assistant takes in an hour; it's far less easy to judge what the quality standard of their responses should be. Some jobs lend themselves easily to measured standards. Others, such as jobs in law, education, medicine or research, cannot easily be judged in terms of levels of performance. It should always be possible, however, for you to define a mutually acceptable method of working, level of behaviour or set of results.

THE JOB DESCRIPTION

The result of all this analysis is a job description (or job specification). Most job descriptions have a small number of elements in common:

❑ job title: location; accountable to/responsible for;
❑ overall objective: the reason the job exists;
❑ key result areas;
❑ performance standards.

Writing all this down helps to sharpen the mind. Actions that we express vaguely in speech must become better defined when we see them on paper. Helping your team member to construct their own job description is a powerful way of helping them to clarify their job for themselves.

Some managers see job descriptions as so much wasted paper. As soon as they're complete, they go out of date. They are right: most jobs evolve rapidly and any definition of them is likely to be overtaken by events. You should view job descriptions as dynamic documents, that must be regularly updated. Think of a job description as somewhat like a plan of campaign: it marks out the territory and sets the terms of a person's performance. But, like all plans, it needs to be revisited often. As Eisenhower once famously remarked: 'plans are useless, but planning is indispensable'.

SETTING TARGETS

Targets are priorities or special tasks that the jobholder needs to achieve beyond routine work. They relate specifically to the individual concerned and set goals for them to achieve. You might review performance standards only rarely – perhaps once a year – but targets are set more frequently and change more often.

Why have targets?

'What gets measured gets done.' This simple and by now infamous sentence is both a rationale for setting targets and a warning against relying on them. The overwhelming advantage of targets is that they motivate performance. We saw in Chapter 2 that goals:

❑ direct our attention;
❑ regulate our efforts;
❑ make us more persistent;
❑ help us plan.

Targets (goals by another name) give us something to aim for and something by which to measure our success. This means that targets help people to:

❑ develop;
❑ plan;
❑ change priorities when circumstances change;
❑ improve their performance over time;
❑ make up 'slippages';
❑ innovate;
❑ achieve projects;
❑ exploit new circumstances;
❑ implement new policies;
❑ challenge their own high expectations of themselves.

But targets can also limit people's attention to targeted activities. It's possible that in concentrating on meeting your targets, you neglect whole areas of your work. Typically, targets that empha-size quantity threaten areas of quality (where targets might be dif-ficult to set).

I think that the dangers of *not* having targets outweigh the dangers of setting them. Successful, effective people work towards goals. The alternative is a lack of focus and well-meaning incompetence.

Targets need to be set sensibly. They should reflect the overall objectives of the organization, and be in line with them. Team tar-gets should translate logically into individual targets. It is vital that people agree and commit to the targets that they are set, and that the targets reflect the full range of their action responsibilities.

Introducing targets

'Ask the man who does the job.' So said Dr Deming, the father of the Quality movement (I'm sure he meant 'woman' too). The golden rule is that you should consult the jobholder when you introduce targets. You have little hope of achieving your own tar-gets without the cooperation of your team. You may have respon-sibility for setting jobholders' targets; but you should always ask them what they think they can achieve.

Consultation will improve the quality of targets in four ways:

❏ **Consultation makes for more accurate targets.** The jobholder knows more about the job than you do. They will have a good idea which targets are reasonable.
❏ **Consultation breeds cooperation.** Even if the jobholder is reluctant or sceptical about a target you set, consulting with them – and giving your reasons for your decision – is more likely to result in genuine commitment on their part.
❏ **Consultation increases involvement.** Provided that targets are realistic in their eyes, the jobholder will be more likely to take ownership of the work.

❑ **Consultation maintains good employee relations.** Consulting with individuals over their targets usefully supplements your negotiations with worker representatives, whether unionized or not.

Asking people to accept the idea of targets can be tricky. Targets may be part of a larger change programme in an organization, which some people may see as merely the latest 'management fad'. Some professionals are traditionally hostile to goal-setting, seeing targets as distractions from their real work. Education and medicine are two areas, for example, where practitioners have demonstrated profound resistance to the idea of targets. In other cultures and professions, targets are seen as somewhat 'downmarket': degrading and beneath people's dignity. And there will always be people who argue that targets cannot be set for their jobs because they are entirely reactive: receptionists or cell workers on an assembly line, for instance, whose activity is dependent almost entirely on external factors.

Then there are the cynics. They may object that:

❑ they are being made to work harder for no extra money;
❑ taking on targets inevitably means taking the blame when it all goes wrong;
❑ these new-fangled targets ride roughshod over established practices and agreements;
❑ their time is being wasted by having to do irrelevant things;
❑ management are moving the goalposts – yet again.

How do you convince the unbelievers? It is vital that people know specifically how their contribution affects larger objectives. If they can see that their work is part of a larger drive towards achievement, they will be more likely to see that their targets make sense.

Remember some basic rules of conversation. Asking questions and listening to the answers may prepare you to be more persuasive than simply telling the jobholder what they should expect.

Start perhaps by asking: 'How would you recognize a good week at work?', 'Name the four or five things by which you would measure or judge success.'

Only the most hardened cynic will claim that it doesn't matter to them whether they've achieved anything at work or not. Most people want to do a good job. And most people want to make a contribution. Showing the nature of that contribution is key to convincing them of the benefits of targets. People's experience of success nearly always relates in some way to the goals of the organization. You should be able to evaluate the jobholder's answers in terms of the key result areas that you have established for their work.

Reassure them that this is *not* a mechanical exercise in time and motion but a genuine attempt to set our sights on the future and improve everybody's performance. None of us achieve all our goals all the time; sometimes we hit targets just a little too easily. Hence the need for constant review and adjustment. Be quite open in calling it 'moving the goalposts'. We live in a world where goalposts move all the time.

How to set targets

Theoretically, target setting starts with the top management team and ends with people who have no managerial responsibility. But it might be dangerous to wait until higher-level targets have been set before setting your own. You can always adjust your own and your team's targets as the pieces arrive from higher management.

Start with your own targets. Decide who is involved in achieving them. Identify the key players and the key result areas where their targets must be set.

SETTING TARGETS: KEY QUESTIONS

❑ What are the business priorities for the coming period?
❑ Who is involved?
❑ What must I do myself?
❑ What must the team do?
❑ What must we ask other people to do?
❑ What are the specific actions to be carried out? By when?
❑ Whose action responsibilities do these fall under?
❑ What organizational goals will our targets support?
❑ What customer goals must we support (internal *and* external)?
❑ What are the targets we must set to achieve our objectives?

Many people know the acronym SMART as applied to targets. It's as good a checklist as any for the targets you will be setting. Make sure that your targets are:

❑ specific;
❑ measurable;
❑ achievable;
❑ realistic;
❑ time-related.

Keep the paperwork simple. You should only need to use one piece of paper on which all goals and targets are recorded, and which you can use to develop competencies and development plans. Keep two copies: one for you and one for the jobholder.

If you use a form, think of it simply as a tool to help you and the jobholder record achievements and discussion. Allow people to scribble all over it if they want to. It's not a formal record of achievement: it's their management tool. You will probably want to start a new target form at each review or appraisal.

Frequently asked questions

Managers who are new to targets seem to ask five main questions:

'How many targets?'
It varies. If you set more than about six, you probably won't hit them all. The number you set will reflect their difficulty and the time span you are working in, but you needn't spread them rigorously over each key result area. Attack the areas of greatest need.

'How much detail?'
Your targets should be precise enough to avoid arguments later! But you might well not state methods as well as goals. Allow the jobholder to exercise their initiative.

'How long should each target last?'
There's no magic time-limit. You should consider staggering deadlines. Most of us can only complete one major target close to deadline. If the jobholder is trying to hit several targets at once, quality may well suffer.

The time-span could be anything from a day to a year. Longer-term targets might well be called goals or objectives. Shorter time-limits are more likely to inspire enthusiasm and energy. At first-line manager or supervisory level, consider time-limits of between two weeks and two months.

'How difficult should targets be?'
One of the main justifications for targets is that they challenge and stretch people. But the jobholder should not perceive them to be impossible or unfairly hard. Look back at the material on goals in Chapter 2.

You may need to tone down the jobholder's enthusiasm in setting a difficult target. Some of us leap at challenges too fast, only to regret it later – and those around us can share the unpleasant consequences of our taking on too much.

'What about changing the target?'
You need to be flexible. Don't change a target without good reason, and without letting the jobholder know the reason.

REVIEWING TARGETS: KEY QUESTIONS

- ❏ How significant is this target in terms of larger organizational objectives?
- ❏ How urgent is this target?
- ❏ How clearly is this target described?
- ❏ How measurable is the target? Are we measuring it accurately or appropriately?
- ❏ Will achieving the target create a real result, or is it only a description of an activity?
- ❏ How stretching is the target?

External factors can change the priority or measure of a target. If you are faced with a problem, your task as a manager is to work out what to do to overcome the problem and realign your targets. In particular, don't drop targets in a crisis. But there's nothing amiss with agreeing that you both got a target wrong. Simply reassess the situation and put things right.

COMPETENCIES

Goals and targets are the outputs of a job. They are 'what to do'. Competencies are the inputs: the 'how to do' skills. People bring competencies to jobs. Understanding the competencies necessary for a job is an important factor in getting the job done well, and it sets the scene for the second element of managing people: how to develop them.

A competency is a behavioural skill. You can demonstrate a competency; it's clear when a competency is successful. Competencies can be seen, evaluated and modified by development. They are *not* character or personality traits. Neither are they a measure of attitude.

Competencies are increasingly fashionable but they are not always well defined. We could define a broad competency – for example, 'driving a car safely' – by breaking it down into smaller, more specific skills: 'changing gear while in motion', 'negotiating a roundabout in line with Highway Code guidelines', and so on. Many competencies remain resistant to easy definition. Many of the most important rely on subtle application of sensitive principles. Many statements and lists of competencies therefore tend to include elements of knowledge, understanding and personal attributes. It's in these important areas that competencies can become unclear and must be handled with care.

There are many consultancies and packages that can help you define and identify competencies. But you can start with the key result areas of the job concerned. Most jobs require between ten and twenty. Targets and competencies are also closely linked. If a jobholder repeatedly misses deadlines and loses documentation, perhaps they lack planning skills. If they continually annoy customers, they are probably lacking interpersonal or customer care skills. Assessing competency begins with assessing what the jobholder needs to achieve in terms of performance standards, and what they might achieve in aiming at a specific target.

Developing competencies is not a strategy to produce company 'clones'. Behaviour will always resist being standardized, as will people's views on assessing it. You do need to be able to agree broadly what competencies mean and on whether or not they can be – and are being – demonstrated.

Typical competencies (these are taken from a food manufacturer) might include:

❑ planning;
❑ problem-solving;

- budgetary control;
- setting objectives;
- face-to-face communication;
- written communication;
- developing individuals;
- team-building;
- customer relationships;
- self-development.

Note how these competencies reflect both the action-centred leadership model – achieving objectives, developing individuals, building the team – and the five-way management model that recognizes a manager's responsibilities upward, downward, across the organization, beyond the organization and to themselves. Against each competency, the manager might be rated on a scale of one to six, or assessed as 'not yet competent', 'competent' or 'more than competent'.

DEFINING A COMPETENCY

Here is an example of a closely-defined competency. It was drawn up through a programme of consultation with managers in a retail company.

Planning and forecasting

To be competent a manager must be able to:

- handle and understand management data;
- carry responsibility and accountability for all the assets under his or her control.

This will involve:

- balancing the needs of the department with the overall needs of the company;

❏ putting forward initiatives on the use of assets, property, plant, equipment, etc;
❏ chasing other departments who must provide input to obtain the required results.

Managers producing the best performance are those who:

❏ identify the needs and resources that are required;
❏ implement plans and control work;
❏ take decisions on the deployment of staff;
❏ minimize downtime, inconvenience to customers and loss of revenue;
❏ plan and carry through medium- and long-term strategies;
❏ recognize the implications and knock-on effects of decisions;
❏ turn overall objectives and standards into individual targets.

It will be clear that assessing competencies can easily become a form-filling, box-ticking exercise. To work well, the competencies must be closely defined and performance carefully monitored.

REVIEWING PERFORMANCE

A performance review is a conversation that many managers would rather not hold. The potential for unpleasantness – or the need to assert your authority – may be too high. Such managers may call for written monthly reports instead. They may justify this practice by saying that 'monthlies' give them a permanent record and save time. In many cases, these reports are merely excuses from facing up to their responsibility. (They are probably also asking their 'direct reports' to spend too much time on unnecessary paperwork.)

Reviewing performance *with the jobholder* is an essential part of your work as a manager. The people who report to you will expect you to check their achievements against standards and targets. If any of your team ever has reason to say 'My manager doesn't even know what I do', you are not discharging this fundamental responsibility of reviewing their performance.

The way you monitor performance is something you should discuss with people as you set their targets. Nobody should be taken by surprise. Exactly how much you monitor is a matter for sensitivity and judgement: it's a good example of a competency that isn't easy to define. You need to establish a balance between setting them free and keeping an eye on how they're doing.

Reviewing performance is not just a matter of measurement. You need to make sure that targets are being achieved – and that you are helping to set reasonable ones. But you are also monitoring the whole performance of the whole person. You can't do this simply by calling for bits of paper. You need to hold conversations.

Neither is performance review a single operation that you conduct once a year. It takes three main forms:

❑ walking the job;
❑ one-to-one reviews;
❑ formal appraisal.

A competent manager will do all three. The form of the review will change in each case.

Walking the job

You should stay in touch. And you should be seen to stay in touch. Regular contact between you and your team is as important as regular contact with your customers or suppliers.

The traditional jargon for this is 'walking the job'. It means setting time aside to visit the team at work, to be with them informally. It gives them the opportunity to talk to you about problems, ideas and achievements. It gives you the chance to see them at work and experience the problems at the sharp end.

For you, walking the job is an opportunity for you to develop your leadership skills. It puts you directly in touch and allows people to give you their views off the cuff. It establishes a reputation for being interested, committed, approachable and understanding. It allows you to thank and praise people. Above all, it allows you to monitor their performance as they are working.

By walking the job regularly, you will quickly establish the expectation that you are there to manage – not to check up, to spy or to catch people out. It's a way of building trust between you and the people who report to you.

WALKING THE JOB: EXAMPLE

The headmaster of our daughter's school is an excellent example of a leader who makes most of his impact by walking the job. He is rarely in his office. He is walking the corridors at the start and end of the day; he is aware of hotspots and is likely to be there to lend a hand. He may walk into a teacher's room at any time. His team expects this and welcomes it. They know that he believes in the excellence of their work and will always give them total support while they are at work. They also know that he is monitoring their performance and is ready to give help or advice. His management style is open, honest and trusting. He manages by walking about.

Walking the job can seem a little forced and artificial to begin with. It's difficult to lay down rigid rules for such an informal management activity. A few simple principles, though, should suffice to help you turn walking the job into your core managerial activity:

❑ do it regularly;
❑ be honest;
❑ be positive.

WALKING THE JOB: DOS AND DON'TS

DO:

❑ set aside time for getting out into the workplace;
❑ turn up when you say you will;
❑ make clear your interests and reasons for being there;
❑ dress appropriately – you may be walking the job 'up a pole' or 'down a hole';
❑ plan to cover every area of responsibility within a defined period, particularly where your team's work involves external customers;
❑ find out in advance if there are any particular topics of interest or concern to the people you will meet;
❑ introduce yourself to new team members;
❑ speak to different team members each time;
❑ speak to everybody over time;
❑ ask questions primarily about work and customers;
❑ be positive and encouraging;
❑ use the person's first name;
❑ respond sympathetically to 'whinges' but steer them towards conversations for opportunity and action;
❑ have a disciplined routine for following up issues;
❑ hold routine meetings with your people at their workplace rather than in your office;
❑ speak your mind: your people expect your leadership;
❑ listen and smile.

DON'T:

❑ always speak to the same people;
❑ answer questions on issues that should first have been raised through line managers;

❑ allow individuals to let off steam on potentially disruptive issues;
❑ give an answer to a question if you are not sure that you are right or if you are breaching confidentiality;
❑ appear to be fault-spotting;
❑ single out trades union representatives for individual discussion on each visit;
❑ appear to be in a hurry to move on;
❑ raise people's expectations unfairly or prematurely;
❑ criticize people in front of others;
❑ tell people what to do;
❑ walk the job with a group of your colleagues.

Monitoring performance against targets

Make sure you hold regular one-to-one conversations with each team member: to review targets, to monitor activities, and to formalize feedback. These are more formal conversations than those you hold walking the job. You should hold them at least monthly, and preferably fortnightly.

Performance reviews of this kind sit comfortably between the informal conversations you hold every day and the most formal of reviews, the appraisal. This – usually annual – performance review too often degenerates into a bureaucratic ritual. Appraisals give you and the jobholder the opportunity to review progress over a long period, but will improve if supported by these more frequent one-to-ones.

This conversation, a semi-formal interview, will benefit from being structured according to the WASP principles we have discussed in Chapter 1:

❑ **Welcome** the jobholder and review your mutual relationship to the work in hand.

- What are the successes of the past week or so?
- Have targets been met? If so, what can we learn from the experience?
- Have any targets not been met?

❑ **Acquire** new information that the jobholder has not had a chance to cover in any informal conversations. Remember that this part of the conversation is also an opportunity for you to assess possibilities: how things might be going wrong, how they could be improved, what the jobholder's feelings might be below the surface.

- If targets have not been met, why? Failure on the jobholder's part? Failure on your part? The jobholder may have left things too late or been overtaken by events; you may have set targets inappropriately, not provided sufficient resources or not explained the target clearly.
- How is the jobholder doing in relation to the more routine parts of the job? Are any standards slipping – or being exceeded?

❑ **Supply** updates on broader issues and how they might be affecting the jobholder's work: existing targets and new opportunities for involvement.

- Should we extend deadlines for targets not yet met, find alternative methods or drop the target altogether?
- Are new issues arising that mean we need to set different objectives and targets?

❑ **Part** by praising achievement, thanking the jobholder for their continued commitment and agreeing any new action points or issues that need particular attention during the next few weeks.

- Summarize how things seem to you to be going; ask them for their opinion. Point the way to the future.

Appraisal

Appraisal is the most formal form of performance review. It usually forms part of a larger employee management scheme, usually administered by a Personnel or Human Resources department. Appraisal is well established in some organizations, and still almost unheard of in others. Appraisal carries three main benefits:

❑ **Appraisal benefits the jobholder.** It gives the jobholder the chance to discuss every aspect of the job, in depth, and away from the pressure of daily work. It clarifies for the jobholder how they are continuing to contribute to the team, to the department and to the wider organization. Appraisal gives clear direction on what is expected in the job and gives the jobholder the opportunity to become involved in planning their work and their future. It's also a long, hard look at competencies both growing and underdeveloped. Appraisal also allows the jobholder to reflect on and discuss how other people influence their work – in particular, of course, their manager! And regular appraisal, with its permanent recording system, should make the jobholder's life and work easier if you, their manager, move on. Finally, appraisal is the major opportunity to create action plans and rededicate the jobholder to the job.

❑ **Appraisal benefits the manager.** It gives you the opportunity to think seriously about how you manage the jobholder. What do you expect of them? Are you using their energies and abilities as well as you can? How can you help them? What training would be useful? What are the jobholder's aspirations? Appraisal allows you to respond formally to success and to talk about problems in an open way. Appraisal is the chance for you to strengthen your managerial relationship with the jobholder and your position as a manager. It should also help you identify skills shortages and plan promotions and replacements. So appraisal is as much an opportunity for you to develop as it is for the jobholder.

❑ **Appraisal benefits the organization.** The appraisal system is the organization's visible commitment to its employees. It shows that the organization wants to involve people in their own work and cares about their morale. It also suggests to potential employees that they will be treated with respect. Appraisal helps the organization plan projects, future resource requirements and promotion (or 'succession'). Used well, appraisal can help to change inflexible organizational structures, to cut out overlaps, to strengthen areas of managerial weakness or confusion and to influence policy.

You may find conducting an appraisal one of the most daunting of your responsibilities as a manager of people. To begin with, you may dislike the idea of appraising a colleague's work face-to-face. The potential for simple embarrassment or hostility blinds many managers to the deeper dangers that underlie appraisal.

The essential elements of an appraisal are *judging performance* and *reporting performance*. Appraisal is not simply measuring performance according to some set of scales; it is the skilful judgement of performance. It's a human activity, not a mechanical one: it involves discretion, discrimination (in the best sense of the word: the ability to distinguish different circumstances and factors and take them into account) and sensitivity. As a manager, you need to make the judgement and communicate it to the jobholder – and, perhaps, to others – so that everybody understands it clearly and can act on it.

Many modern appraisal systems include an element of self-appraisal. This makes the jobholder's involvement in the process explicit by permanently recording their own views. Other new initiatives include peer assessment – appraisal by the team rather than by an individual manager – and 360-degree appraisal, which usually means that the jobholder – or team as a whole – are able to appraise their manager. Logically, such a form of appraisal might extend to include customers: regular or occasional contacts both inside and outside the organization. In practice, this might mean monitoring phone calls in a call centre or asking customers to fill out satisfaction forms. The jobholders may find themselves being assessed on the basis of portfolios of work, worksheets or rotas, or even external assessment systems supplied by consultancies.

WHAT MAKES AN APPRAISAL GO WRONG?

These are the main danger points for any manager in an appraisal. Become aware of these and you are already well on the way to conducting more effective appraisals:

- ❏ negative prejudice;
- ❏ lack of knowledge about the jobholder;
- ❏ lack of knowledge about the job;
- ❏ the halo effect: simply liking the jobholder or getting on with them;
- ❏ failure to distinguish performance from the circumstances surrounding the job;
- ❏ differing perceptions between manager and jobholder of job definition, standards of appraisal or criteria for judgement;
- ❏ marking everybody 'just above average';
- ❏ ignoring the outcome of the appraisal: for example, not acting on commitments made in the appraisal to improve resources, training or procedures.

You may also be concerned about the appraisal system that your organization operates. This can range from having no system at all, through the tradition of an informal chat once a year, to a full-blown ritual of form-filling and grading for pay awards. You may also have to manage the wider range of responses and attitudes towards appraisal that exist in certain sectors and professions. Teaching is an example of a profession where appraisal has become virtually a political issue.

Appraisal systems tend to fall into one of three main types:

- ❏ **Grading or merit rating.** This method usually involves listing certain criteria and then awarding grades: for example, *excellent, very good, good, fair, poor.* The criteria vary enormously from scheme to scheme: examples might include *reliability, drive, flexibility;* or *honesty, communication, initiative, cooperation, integrity.* They might be related to identified competencies required for the job. You and the jobholder might even have the power to choose the criteria by which to judge performance.

The method has a number of disadvantages: it is backward-looking, forces the jobholder into a reactive position and is very vulnerable to subjective judgement. If appraisal is linked to salary review, you may be tempted to be over-generous in your assessment. Because it is an easy method to use, it encourages managers to be lazy in appraising people. Gradings often reflect the relationship between manager and jobholder rather than actual achievement.

If you find yourself using a grading system, you should aim to:
- support your grades with written comments;
- define the criteria and the words or numbers used for rating;
- take jobholders' comments into account;
- agree your ratings rather than impose them;
- expand your performance review so that grading becomes only one part;
- relate your judgements to performance and not personality.

❑ **Written assessment.** The big difference between written assessment and simple grading is that you will have to write your judgements down in sentences and not just mark or tick boxes. The great advantage is that you can give more thought to what you want to say and how to say it. The main disadvantage of the system is that it may display more about your writing skills than the jobholder's performance. Managers operating this system often worry about their ability to put subtle judgements into prose. Of course, those judgements still depend on your choice of criteria by which to define performance and your choice of values by which to judge it. Without the predetermined categories of grading, these can become even more subjective. You may also be tempted to write the appraisal without talking to the jobholder – thus rendering the entire process meaningless.

If you are using written assessments, you should aim to:
- make your judgements specific and substantive (supported by objective evidence);
- make your criteria of judgement explicit;
- base your assessment on a conversation with the jobholder;
- give the jobholder the chance to think about some key questions before the conversation.

❏ **Integrated performance management.** This might be called Management by Objectives (MBO). To minimize the problems associated with subjective judgement, some organizations have tied appraisal into a larger system of performance management. The advantage of such a system is that appraisal becomes clearly linked to job descriptions, organizational objectives, individual targets, development plans and reward or pay systems.

The great danger of such integrated systems is bureaucracy. Appraisal remains a matter of personal judgement, and those who try to systematize the process inevitably want to make judgements and reporting practices as consistent as possible. Increased paperwork is almost inevitably the result.

If you are appraising within a larger performance management system, you should aim to:
- understand the system as fully as possible;
- understand all the criteria of judgement and any grading scales clearly;
- judge performance according to agreed measures or standards;
- find ways of including your own judgement in the appraisal (through written comments);
- include the jobholder in all aspects of appraisal;
- appraise the work and not the person.

Appraisal often suffers by being linked to conversations about pay. The problem is that the perceived link can distract both your and the jobholder's attention from the real business of appraisal.

It can even threaten the openness and honesty of the conversation. You might be tempted to raise your judgements in order to avoid conflict; jobholders may try to bargain down their targets in order to inflate the award next time.

Conversations about salary should be separate from appraisal. Salary is recognition of past performance; appraisal is principally a conversation about the future. If you *must* make a recommendation about salary on the appraisal form, base it clearly on performance and achievement against clearly understood standards, objectives and targets. Allow the jobholder to be involved.

You need to appreciate the particular strengths and weaknesses of the appraisal system that your organization operates. Where appraisal fails – and it does, all too often – it may be because the system is creaky, or because the appraising manager feels uncomfortable with the process.

CONDUCTING AN APPRAISAL

An appraisal interview is one of the most important conversations you hold as a manager. It must involve all the skills of conversation we have looked at in Chapter 1. And it's also vital that both you and the jobholder prepare thoroughly for the interview.

Preparing for the interview

You should study the jobholder's job description and the standards of performance you have set up. If targets have been set and regularly reviewed, think about these with care. The key questions to ask at this stage are:

❑ What results has the jobholder achieved?
❑ Where has the jobholder exceeded expectations or shown real progress?
❑ Which results have not been achieved? Can you suggest why?

Make sure that you tell the jobholder what you are doing to prepare and invite them to prepare in a similar way.

Ask them, well in advance, to consider their own performance over the appraised period and to note successes, failure and anything in between! Ask them to think also about how circumstances have affected their performance in general and in achieving particular tasks or targets. Has the job altered? Do they think that the job description should be reviewed? The jobholder should also think about possibilities of job development: chances for greater responsibility, for training or some other kind of learning programme, perhaps towards a qualification. What are their ambitions and aspirations? Ask them also to consider how they have been managed during the period and what they might like to see improved in *your* performance as their manager.

The essence of a successful appraisal is the comparison of the two sets of ideas: yours and the jobholder's. You are aiming for shared understanding: an agreement about the jobholder's performance and potential for the future. The conversation is unlikely to be successful without a high degree of mutual trust and respect. This is only partly something that you as an individual manager can work towards. If the culture of your organization doesn't value these qualities, appraisal will become difficult and possibly self-defeating.

JOBHOLDER'S CHECKLIST

You could offer this list of questions to the jobholder to help them assess their own performance before the appraisal interview:

1. Are you sure of the boundaries of the job?

   – Is there any overlap with another's action responsibilities?

   – Is there any uncertainty about your own action responsibility: where you're not sure whether you should take the responsibility or not?
   – Are there any areas of 'no responsibility' that you are aware of: where nobody seems to be accountable?

2. Are you sure of your exact authority?

   – Where are the limits of your authority?
   – Are the limits problematic or difficult?
   – Where would you like more authority to make decisions?

3. How have you done recently?

   – Have you achieved against performance standards?
   – Have you met your targets?

4. What's hindering your performance?

   – External circumstances?
   – Other people or teams?
   – Budgetary constraints?
   – Administrative resources (lack of or poor)?
   – Communication difficulties?
   – Lack of knowledge?
   – Physical constraints: access, office space, poor machine maintenance...?

5. Do you have adequate knowledge of your targets?
6. What do you want to do next? Development aspirations, training, new challenges...?
7. What help do you need? Where could it come from? Specifically, can your appraising manager help you further? How can the team help?

As manager, you have a responsibility to ensure that the appraisal interview is of a high quality. Prepare by allocating an appropriate **place** and **length of time** for the conversation to take place.

The interview should happen in a comfortable and private space, with the minimum of distractions. Your office may well not be the best place to put the jobholder at ease. Think about how you can arrange the furniture to encourage the supportive and cooperative style of conversation you will need.

How can you manage the timings of your appraisal? Allocate more than sufficient time – especially if you guess that a particular appraisal will need it. Make sure that you are not conducting too many in one day. The system may demand that you conduct appraisals at certain times of year, and this can result in unhelpful bunching. If you cannot avoid this, at least manage your time as well as possible so that you don't appraise more than two people a day.

PREPARING TO APPRAISE; TEN QUESTIONS:

❑ Have you prepared enough?
❑ Have you checked the records?
❑ Have you checked the facts of performance?
❑ Have you worked out your main questions?
❑ Are they open? Use why, how, when, where, who and what.
❑ Have you a strategy and a structure? Are you ready to change it if necessary?
❑ Have you left enough time?
❑ Have you done all you can to make the space comfortable and unthreatening?
❑ Have you got pen and paper for making brief notes?
❑ Have you given instructions not to be disturbed?

Holding the interview

You are aiming to hold a rich and open conversation. It should have seven key features:

- ❑ It's private.
- ❑ The conversation is about the whole job.
- ❑ The meeting is structured. Start with the WASP model and develop that.
- ❑ The conversation is about the past, the present and the future.
- ❑ The meeting's outcomes are recorded.
- ❑ The conversation is about the relationship: it includes both jobholder and manager.
- ❑ The conversation results in specific actions with deadlines and named actioners (not just the jobholder but perhaps you or others too).

You might kill the appraisal off at an early stage by descending into adversarial conversation. Be ready with the ladder of inference to take any potential controversy into a more careful examination of facts and feelings. Let's take our four-stage model of effective conversations and apply it to appraisal:

- ❑ **Welcome. A conversation for relationship**. Review standards, targets, the job description and any other aspects of performance that you have both looked at. Relate them: take comparisons and talk about what's been achieved, and what has not happened. Stick to the known facts and make sure that you agree them.

  Your questions to the jobholder might include:
  - How do you feel your job has been going since we last spoke?
  - What do you feel you do best?
  - Where do you have real problems?
  - How relevant is the job description?

❑ **Acquire. A conversation for possibility.** Open up the conversation by asking the jobholder for their views and withholding your own. Review the possible reasons for achievement or lack of it. Open up the conversation to include matters of competency, skills, training and external circumstances.

Questions at this stage might include:
 – What are your strong points?
 – Where do you think you could develop?
 – What particular problems have you had? How do you think you could have handled them differently?

Look for possibilities rather than uttering closed judgements. Instead of saying, for example, 'You're aggressive with our customers', you might say 'Some of our customers seem to perceive your behaviour as aggressive. What do you think about that?' Use behaviour as the basis for your comments. Have evidence to hand. Be ready to reinterpret the evidence from the jobholder's point of view. Use the ladder of inference.

❑ **Supply. A conversation for opportunity.** This is the problem-solving part of the conversation. Analyse what you have found and focus on opportunities for action, change and improvement. Generate alternatives. Seek agreement on what could be done. You might be looking for new moves towards targets, performance standards or even amendments to the job description.

Questions at this stage include:
 – 'What might we do to alter our targets or standards?'
 – 'Do we need to rewrite any part of the job description?'
 – 'How could the job be improved? Have you any ideas?'

❑ **Part. A conversation for action.** You and the jobholder confirm your agreement and part on the clear understanding that these actions are recorded and will be monitored.

Look back at the essential elements of a conversation for action. Remember that you will gain more commitment from the jobholder if you make requests and invite them to a considered response.

Don't complete any forms during the interview. It will take too long and distract you from the real business of the conversation. Take time to fill out any paperwork carefully, at some point after the conversation has ended. You need time to assemble your thoughts and summarize them in your mind. You should, of course, show any completed paperwork to the jobholder and involve them in any changes.

Make sure that you carry out any actions that you agree in the interview: support, procedural changes, delegation or training. If you do not, you undermine both your own authority and the credibility of the appraisal process itself. And you will find it harder next time to generate the respect and trust that form the basis of the whole system.

Identifying development needs

Managing a person's performance is really about both *outputs* and *inputs*. The outputs are what the jobholder achieves to contribute to the organization's objectives; the inputs are the jobholder's skills and competencies.

Identifying a jobholder's development needs is therefore a balance between these two concerns: developing the person on the one hand, and investing in the organization's future on the other.

People can develop continuously. Appraisal is the ideal opportunity for you to monitor that progress and refocus it. Bear these key points in mind as you appraise:

❑ Identify the needs as accurately as possible.
❑ Try never to talk about 'weaknesses'. They are 'areas for development'.
❑ Create situations and opportunities to practise competencies and develop new ones.
❑ Not all development needs to be fulfilled by training. Offer coaching and, if necessary, counselling. And there are many other ways in which people can learn more cheaply, easily, effectively and quickly.

This part of the appraisal conversation may well lead to a more formal training needs analysis or a development plan. We consider this whole area of managerial responsibility in the next chapter.

Handling poor performance

At some point you will have to handle poor performance. Everybody performs under par at times. Usually we can tolerate some underachieving but persistent or serious shortfalls need action. Avoiding the issue will not make it go away.

What you see as poor performance is not necessarily the jobholder's fault. In fact, it's unrewarding to think in terms of blame if you detect poor performance. Many organizations find it hard to shrug off a 'blame culture' and you may find yourself infected with it – particularly if you have been a victim of it. Of course, it may be a genuine case of misconduct; but the circumstances of poor performance are likely to be more complex. An effective manager will look deeper and not jump to conclusions.

So how do you handle those situations where performance falls short of your expectations? What do you do if the shortfall is habitual? The appraisal interview is only one of the opportunities to tackle the issue.

First, establish the gap. What is the standard that isn't being met? It may be in the job description, but standards of performance may also be contained in:

❑ contracts of employment;
❑ rulebooks;
❑ training manuals;
❑ lists of standards;
❑ procedures;
❑ minutes of team briefings;
❑ training sessions;
❑ records of conversations.

Somebody may be having difficulties with any of these sources of standards. Procedures are often not well written; minutes of briefings may not be accurate. Any information can be hidden or poorly communicated.

For records of actual performance, you might look at:

❑ personal files;
❑ time sheets;
❑ sickness and absence records;
❑ record cards;
❑ customer complaints;
❑ examples of inaccurate work;
❑ records of mistakes;
❑ comparison with others' work;
❑ examples of unfinished work.

Establish the required standard and look at the record of performance. Is the gap sufficient enough, and consistent enough, to warrant action?

Now you need to establish possible reasons for the gap in achievement. Some managers would suggest that poor performance is because the jobholder is either incapable (in which case it's a training issue) or unwilling (which makes the matter presumably a reward issue – re-enter Maslow…). Of course, there is a third possibility: you. A key factor in anybody's performance is their manager's performance. Shortfalls in performance put you under scrutiny too, because you are responsible in the wider organization for setting standards, agreeing competencies and designing the work.

Reasons for underperformance

There are three main reasons why jobholders can underperform:

❑ **Domestic circumstances.** The jobholder may not have the skills necessary to do the job. They may be in poor health or suffering some emotional instability that is due to family or personal problems.

❑ **Poor management.** The job has not been sufficiently explained. Planning has been poor. The job may have changed in ways that don't make sense to the jobholder. Resources may be lacking. Discipline may be slack. Physical conditions may make working to standard very difficult. You may be managing the job poorly – as may another manager.

❑ **Lack of organizational fit.** The jobholder may be unhappy in the team, or the team unhappy with them. So-called 'personality clashes' may be getting in the way, or a sense of natural justice may be being abused. The jobholder's personal, moral, religious or political values may be in conflict with those of others. They may be lacking in confidence or unable to adopt the wider values of the team or the organization.

Poor performance usually leads to the need for some form of counselling. This isn't necessarily the complicated psychological technique the name suggests. Counselling is simply helping people to find out for themselves how to overcome problems. You need to encourage the jobholder to think their way towards their own solution. Only they can change their behaviour. Your job is not to offer a solution, unless you are asked.

The right word in the right tone of voice may be all that is needed to put things right. If the conversation needs to become more formal, within the appraisal for example, use the four-part structure to help you through it.

❑ Focus on the problem. Ask about how the jobholder sees it. This is not unlike looking for symptoms of a disease. You must establish with them that a gap or problem exists. Make it clear that this is a problem for you as their manager, and you want to help.

❑ Ask whether they understand the nature of the problem, and whether they can offer any kind of explanation. Ask them how they feel about it. Listen carefully. Did we set the targets right? Are the standards inappropriate or in conflict with others? Is a lack of skill at the core of the problem? Is training necessary – or more practice? Has the job been badly designed? Has it become out of place in some rearrangement of responsibilities?

Other possibilities are that the jobholder feels penalized for doing things right and so is doing what actually gets results or job satisfaction. You may need to remove the cause of this sense of being penalized: overly bureaucratic procedures, for example. Or they may actually be doing very good work but ignoring targets. Or they may feel that the particular standard in question is not important (many of us – often the most committed of us – can feel like this about many standards of performance at work). Emphasize the importance of performing to standard.

❑ Explore with the jobholder opportunities for improvement. Where might they exist? What possible courses of action are open to us? How might you be able to help? Think of this as a joint problem-solving session, in which the jobholder is leading the thinking, with you helping and guiding. Resist the temptation to tell the jobholder what he or she should do.

❑ Find a course of action that the jobholder can agree to. Only they can behave differently, so they must decide on what to do. They may not be able to solve the problem in one go. Many shortfalls in performance – rather like debts – can be resolved in stages. Explain that you are available to help, that you will be reviewing performance over the next few weeks, and that this matter will be recorded.

DEVELOPING PEOPLE

You cannot afford not to develop the people you manage. To make their fullest possible contribution, they need to feel that:

❑ they are getting personal satisfaction from their work;
❑ they are making a worthwhile contribution to their team and their organization;
❑ they find their work challenging;
❑ they have a degree of responsibility that they can handle comfortably;
❑ their contribution is recognized (and, perhaps, rewarded);
❑ they have genuine control over those aspects of their work for which they are responsible;
❑ their work is helping them to develop and grow in experience, ability and maturity.

This is perhaps the one managerial responsibility that you are in most danger of ignoring. Jobs need to be done, and teams are often difficult to avoid simply because there are more of them than of you! But an individual's development may not form the centre of your attention. After all, you aren't in the business of helping them to grow and mature as human beings; your job is to manage them as resources.

WHY DEVELOP PEOPLE?

The simple answer is that, if you don't, you may lose them. Organizations that don't provide for the expectations of skilled people are likely to find themselves with unskilled or non-existent staff. Put more positively, developed people are more valuable resources. You get more out of them for your money! And developing existing staff is also much more cost-efficient than recruiting and inducting new employees. Investing in people and their development brings any organization reduced running costs and greater customer satisfaction.

The really difficult decision is how much to invest in developing people. The greater the investment, the more employable you make somebody, and the more attractive they become to the competition. Every organization has to make the choice between investing in people and the risk of losing the investment.

From your more immediate point of view, developing a person at work helps them to do their work more competently. This increases both their own productivity and that of the organization. Develop somebody's skills and you will achieve:

❑ greater productivity in less time, because people will work more safely, more efficiently, more closely to standards and with minimum waste and damage;
❑ improved job performance, in terms of increased output, improved quality, and timeliness;
❑ greater empowerment: people are better prepared to take on delegated tasks and wider responsibility, they will be more motivated and absenteeism and accidents will decline;
❑ more satisfactory recruitment and selection: the prospect of developing in the job will attract more and better applicants;
❑ reduced labour turnover: at least in theory, people will stay in jobs where they see a prospect of growing and developing their potential.

You can look on this responsibility to nurture people's development as being very like parenting. Some managers are very dogmatic and strict: 'Do it like I do.' Others are more facilitating and encourage people to find their own direction and assess their own development. If you have experienced good parenting, you are likely to develop into a mature, confident, self-possessed and self-developing individual. Similarly, if you 'parent' your team in an empowering and caring way, they are likely to become successful and confident team members. Apart from the satisfaction of having had a part in someone else's development, this positive attitude to others' development helps *you* to perform better and make a more worthwhile contribution.

Development very often means training – and training, all too often, means courses. But development is potentially a much wider and richer process than simply attending training courses. Learning – real, lifelong learning – can happen in a wide variety of ways, settings, relationships and conversations. In this chapter, we look at some of the more common ways in which you can help your team members to develop and learn.

HOW TO ASSESS POTENTIAL

Development potential can be identified in a number of ways:

❑ Appraisal identifies what training and development activities are appropriate to the planned work of the next year.
❑ Changes in a team or department may result in a programme of training and development for the whole team.
❑ An individual jobholder may wish to improve their abilities for current work or future prospects.
❑ Development may begin to take place as part of the systematic progress of induction and initial training.
❑ An individual or team may start a formal programme of development as part of a recovery strategy.

❑ Development may be built into a career structure or a person's contract of employment. This is often called 'continuing professional development' or CPD. The jobholder is required to show evidence of a certain number of days devoted to development in a year.

THE DEVELOPMENT PROCESS

The development process involves deciding what competencies, skills or knowledge need to be developed, and how to go about achieving this. As with most managerial decisions, you will have to make this one on the basis of the resources and opportunities available. There's no point in planning an extensive development programme if resources are likely to run out halfway through. There's no point in sending one of your team on an expensive training course if they have no chance of putting the learnt skills into practice when they come back.

The starting point, then, is to identify jobholders' competency status. Which competencies are necessary for the job? What skills does the jobholder possess that are not employed? Packages designed to complete a training needs analysis are available to do this job; but as a competent manager you should be able, with the jobholders, to make a reasonable estimate of what is needed. You could make this analysis more sophisticated by cross-referencing the competencies needed with the key result areas of the team's or organization's objectives. Those competencies that align to an important key result area gain importance.

You might categorize each competence for a jobholder under three categories. In each, you can decide that the jobholder is:

❑ not yet competent;
❑ fully competent;
❑ more than competent.

For each category, you can consider these possible courses of action:

DEVELOPING NEEDS FROM COMPETENCY ANALYSIS

❑ Not yet competent:
  – Identify areas of weakness.
  – Provide training and development to achieve competence.
❑ Fully competent:
  – Provide training and development for the next stage of competence.
❑ More than competent:
  – Increase opportunities for responsibility and challenge.
  – Promote, reassign work, redesign job.

For those who are not yet competent – the word 'incompetent' is not in the effective manager's vocabulary! – identifying needs and providing opportunities to develop is relatively easy. Similarly, those who are more than competent will probably create their own development paths. It's the middle category who are in most danger of being ignored. Unlike the 'not yet competent', they display no urgent need for development; unlike the 'more than competent', they may not be self-motivated to develop. Unless they can see rewards for achievement that they value, they are unlikely to improve their performance – which is, after all, why we are interested in developing them. You may need to spend some time with these fully competent people to produce a development plan that the jobholder sees as being in their best interests.

Having identified the needs for development, you can draw up a development plan. This is a set of actions designed to improve or consolidate a competency. Make sure that your plan includes SMART actions: specific, measurable, achievable, realistic and – above all – timely. It can be difficult to arrange development or training at the most convenient time, but activities that are too early or too late can lose a great deal of their value. Review development objectives at least once a month.

Incidentally, this work is *not* entirely the work of the Personnel or HR department. You, as the jobholder's manager, must take primary responsibility for holding the development conversation that identifies needs and actions to address them. You know the jobholder best; you best know the needs of the job.

Development is not just training. Many opportunities for development arise within the job. Look around at what the workplace can offer before investing in expensive and time-consuming alternatives. These workplace opportunities can be missed or ignored in the cause of getting the work done. Walking the job is an excellent way to learn about current concerns. You can learn about new opportunities for working arrangements or relationships that you might exploit for development purposes; you may even find that development is taking place, informally, without your involvement.

DELEGATION

Delegation is one of the most immediate ways of offering a development path. It is also, potentially, one of the most cost-effective. It allows people to test their own ideas and develop their understanding and confidence. It is one of the chief means of empowering people.

Delegation is deliberately choosing to give somebody authority to do something you could do yourself. It is not just handing out work. You give somebody a responsibility: the task to be performed; and you devolve authority: the power to make other decisions and to take action to carry out the responsibility. Successful delegation involves matching responsibility with authority.

Anybody who manages will know how difficult this can be – as will any parent or carer.

Delegation is a risk. You retain ultimate accountability. You carry the can; it's your responsibility to answer for any spillages – and to mop them up!

Delegation also brings many rewards. It leaves you free to do your real job; it allows you to look up and ahead, to think more strategically and monitor the progress of your decision. It also generates commitment by involving and motivating people. It can give people greater job satisfaction and develop them by increasing their authority and skills.

What to delegate

Review your own objectives. Identify those for which you are personally accountable. Now distinguish between the activities you can delegate and those for which you must take personal responsibility. Obvious candidates for delegation include:

❑ routine tasks;
❑ time-consuming tasks: research, testing, administrative or coordinating activities;
❑ complete tasks that can be delegated as a block of work;
❑ communication tasks: letters, promotional material, phone calls.

Delegate tasks that might be tedious for you but prove a real challenge to somebody else. A task may be time-consuming because you are not so good at it, or have no new ideas for tackling it. To somebody else, such tasks may be satisfying and rewarding, with opportunities to demonstrate creativity and high performance. Do not delegate:

❑ tasks completely beyond the skills and experience of the person concerned;

❑ strategic, policy, confidential or security matters;
❑ tasks involving discipline over the person's peers.

Beware, too, of using any of these as excuses for not delegating.
There may be other reasons for your unwillingness to delegate:

❑ **Lack of experience.** Someone may appear unsuitable for a
   task but be highly eligible to undertake it, given appropriate
   support and training. It would be unwise to delegate without
   offering support; but the learning challenge might be just
   what makes somebody successful.
❑ **Refusing to let go.** You may enjoy certain tasks, even though
   they do not contribute to your core objectives. You may be
   frightened of letting others take authority for tasks you have
   always carried out in the past.
❑ **Impatience.** Others are bound to do things differently from
   you. They are also likely to get things wrong or seem slow to
   pick up skills. Performance may suffer: when did you last do
   something right first time? On the other hand, a fresh
   approach may actually improve performance. Some managers may be frightened of delegating for precisely this reason.
❑ **Keeping in touch.** Some managers are reluctant to delegate
   because they want to 'keep their finger on the pulse'. At its
   worst, this syndrome means that every decision must be
   referred to them, every letter must be countersigned by them
   and every mistake must be followed by a 'stewards' enquiry' –
   a quasi-judicial meeting at which people are criticized and
   humiliated in front of their colleagues.
❑ **Losing out.** Delegating responsibility and authority may lead
   you to feel that you are grooming your best people to leave,
   that they may be promoted over your head or that you are
   delegating yourself out of a job.

All of these inhibitors can prevent you from delegating successfully. They are effectively preventing you from attending to your
real responsibilities as a manager. Making yourself indispensable

is a reasonable ambition; failing to develop responsibility in others is not a good way of going about it.

How to delegate

Having decided what to delegate, ask:

❑ What skills, experience, expertise and qualifications are necessary for the task?
❑ Whose skills profile best matches the need?
❑ What further training or support would be necessary?

Look for people's interest in work that they haven't done, or have maybe shown some aptitude for in unusual circumstances (covering for somebody else, coping in a crisis). Look for abilities that are exercised elsewhere: in another part of their work, perhaps outside work.

Discuss the prospect of delegating the task to the person you have chosen. This can, of course, conveniently take place at an appraisal interview.

The conversation for delegation should carefully follow the structure of a conversation for action. Begin by making the request. 'I should like to discuss with you the possibility of delegating X.' Explain why you are making the request, both in terms of your need and in terms of the jobholder's development. Give timescales or deadlines, as well as conditions of satisfaction: standards or targets to be achieved, how you will monitor progress and check for success.

Make it clear to the delegate that they have four possible responses:

❑ They can accept the request and make a commitment: 'I promise that I will do X by time Y.'

❑ They can decline. A request is not an order. They must be free to say 'No', while at the same time being clear of the consequences of a refusal.
❑ They can commit to commit later: 'I'll get back to you by time Z, when I will give you a definite response.'
❑ They can make a counter-offer: 'I'm not willing to do X; however, I can promise you to do W (or maybe part of X) by time Y.'

The result of this conversation is a clear commitment by the delegate to action: to the task originally intended for delegation, to part of the task, to another task or to refusal.

In accepting a newly delegated responsibility, the delegate must be clear about three limits on his or her action:

❑ **Objectives.** The broad objectives of the task, the specific targets, conditions of satisfaction and timescale should all be made explicit.
❑ **Policy.** Rules and regulations. The manner in which the task is carried out must conform to any legal, contractual or policy guidelines under which the organization operates.
❑ **Limits of authority.** This is critically important. The delegate must know clearly where their authority extends and where it ends: what powers they have for hiring or using staff, their budgetary authority, the resources available, their access to information and power to take decisions without referral.

Finally, you must give the delegate full confidence to do the task. Make it plain that you will:

❑ give any support that you or they consider necessary;
❑ provide any training that may be needed;
❑ be available for consultation or advice;
❑ make the delegation public knowledge.

All of these commitments are important, but the last two are vitally so. Don't delegate and disappear! You may see delegation as a way of simply turning your back on a difficult problem; if so, you are failing in your responsibilities by landing someone else with the problem. And delegation should always be made public, so that everyone else knows who to turn to in this matter, who is in charge, who they can trust to make the decisions.

Delegation can often itself develop into three other forms of development:

❑ **Acting up.** The delegate takes on a whole role rather than a single task. This is often called temporary cover. But acting up is more than just covering for maternity leave, absence or vacancy. It gives the jobholder the opportunity to broaden their experience and skills in positions of greater responsibility. The difficulty can be that the jobholder can find it hard to return to their original post: re-entry needs careful and sympathetic management, and this is your responsibility.

❑ **Job rotation.** Here, people do different jobs within the section or team – or elsewhere in the organization – over a period of time. Job rotation broadens people's knowledge as well as their skills. Many organizations use job rotation as a managerial development process. The difficulties associated with job rotation are that specialized staff can disappear for periods, leaving work undone, teams are disrupted and quality can suffer.

❑ **Secondments.** A secondment is a placement in another part of the organization – or inside another organization, sometimes abroad – to achieve a specific task. It is often used for managerial or professional development. The danger of course is that the secondee may never return!

Delegation always carries the ultimate risk that you develop a person out of a job. This may create instability in the team, but it also creates new opportunities for development and change.

TRAINING

Training is the planned provision of learning that equips us with skills. It differs from teaching in that it emphasizes improvements in behaviour or performance rather than increasing knowledge. Training should always help you to *do* something rather than *know* something.

Who needs training?

Anybody can be eligible for training, of course. It's normally our circumstances that mark us out as potential trainees.

New employees
Any self-respecting organization will offer induction training to new employees. This familiarizes them with the organization as a whole, its products or services, its polices, and practices. Induction is a critically important form of training, especially for younger people. A single induction programme can influence attitudes to work for a lifetime. The Personnel or Human Resources department may deliver some part of this training. You have a responsibility to introduce new employees to your own department or team, to train them from the start in how the team works and the standards of performance and behaviour you expect from your people.

Jobholders who need to improve performance
Training will also help existing employees who need to maintain standards or improve their competence. Identifying their needs is your responsibility as their manager: it should be the logical result of your monitoring and the appraisal process.

People preparing for promotion
Your organization needs to exploit the talents of its people at every level. Promoting from within is far more efficient than

bringing in new talent from outside. People seeking and expecting promotion will need training in those aspects of their new work that are new to them. This process of 'growing their own' is important in organizations that want to have senior managers in the future who understand the business. Talent-spotting is another of your key responsibilities in this respect.

People moving jobs
Change moves ever more rapidly. Jobs are regularly moved, redesigned and abolished. Flexibility is now perhaps the most valuable quality in an employee. Training makes people better prepared to change direction, take on new responsibilities and respond to the unforeseen.

People nearing retirement
Responsible organizations offer training and induction to those who are about to enter the third age. This sector of the workforce is growing and can offer a wealth of experience and skill. Training can help people maintain standards, consider job moves and other ways of using their skills (in instructing and mentoring, for example), and find new kinds of contribution (as consultants or volunteers).

How to train?

The process should begin, as ever, with an examination of the job and the competencies required to do it. You then need to match the competence or skill to the type of training that you think will help develop it.

You may simply decide that a single skill or competence requires the jobholder to attend a training course. Even such a simple decision becomes more complicated as you explore it. Is the course deliverable in-house, or do you need to find an external provider? Can you do the training yourself – in which case perhaps it will become coaching? How do you know that a training course will provide exactly what you want? This question of matching training to the actual needs of the jobholder must be addressed; you must help the jobholder resolve it. If you don't, the jobholder may become demotivated and you will have lost a substantial investment of budget and time.

Whether for a single training event or for a programme of training, these are the key questions you must ask:

❑ **Who is to be trained?** Is more than one person involved? Can we make more of our investment by involving more people?
❑ **Why are they being trained?** What skills improvements are we looking for?
❑ **What should be taught?** Do we have a 'shopping list' that can translate into a programme or agenda for the training?
❑ **How should the training happen?** More on this in a moment.
❑ **Who should do the training?** You? An internal trainer? An external provider? A teacher from a local college or university? A professional adviser?
❑ **When should it happen?** Length of training? Frequency? Relevance to other initiatives?
❑ **Where should it happen?** The location of the training is surprisingly important. On site? At a training centre or unit? A hotel? A conference centre?
❑ **How do we evaluate the training?**

Find out as much as you can about any training that's on offer. Any reputable training organization will be happy to talk through the work that they do and most will offer to tailor the training to your needs. You must know what those needs are as clearly as possible; talking to a trainer should help you to clarify them.

Training broadly divides into three main types.

On-the-job training
This is probably the most common type of training. It often goes on all the time without even being called training. More formally organized, it allows the trainee to work in a real environment

with support from a skilled person. This gives the trainee real practice and doesn't involve outside trainers or new equipment. Of course, not all experts are skilled trainers. Adequate briefing, feedback and support to help the trainee build on the training are essential.

On-the-job training has a number of key advantages. It is easy to check for relevance and usefulness; it's efficient, in terms of budget and time; it's low-cost and easy to control; it allows for immediate feedback. Its disadvantages include the potential for interruptions, the limited scope of the training and – potentially – the lack of training skill in a skilled person not themselves trained in training.

Off-the-job training
In this kind of training, people from within the organization offer a range of learning events and facilities to support development. These might include short courses, talks, lectures, audio-visual training, distance learning and computer-aided work.

Off-the-job training usually provides a more professional and skilled level of training. It is most often provided by people who have contacts beyond the organization and can provide new and interesting ideas. By taking trainees away from the workplace, off-the-job training encourages greater concentration on the matter in hand. It does carry some dangers, however. The trainer may be from a Training Department or HR Department that is itself cut off from the rest of the organization. The training may be modular and thus vulnerable to remaining uncompleted. Even off the job, people can still be dragged away from training to put things right or fight fires.

Training outside the organization
Training can be provided away from the workplace, at a training centre or hotel. This may be off-the-job training organized from within, or training provided by an external supplier. This kind of training has the potential to make the most difference: hearts and minds can be strongly affected by the cross-fertilization of

experiences on a public training course, by the complete change of scenery and the sense of being able to stand back from the job in a relaxed environment. There are three main dangers in such training: it can be irrelevant because not closely allied to the objectives of the trainee or their organization, it is difficult to control and it is by far the most expensive training option.

Within these three broad categories, many different training methods are available. On-the-job training is likely to be immediate experience doing the work, though the trainer might also decide to include different approaches like conversations about past work, discussion over reports and other documentation, and more informal reflective conversation. A project might count as on-the-job training. Off-the-job training can include a library of resources: this might range from a cupboard full of books to a fully equipped training centre with terminals, on-line facilities and a huge supply of training media. Training outside the organization might be anything from a short course to a development event at an outward-bound centre.

You will know from your own experience of training which type of training makes sense to you. In truth, training – and training providers – vary enormously in approach and quality. Apart from finding out as much as possible about the training itself, you must ensure that it is integrated as quickly and effectively as possible into the trainee's work when they return.

Evaluating training

The most important advice to give about evaluating training is: do it! So many managers use training as an excuse to abdicate from their own development responsibilities. You must be able to justify your investment.

You can begin by asking:

❑ Did the results meet the objectives?
❑ Is there evidence of improved performance?

❑ What benefits have accrued to the team and to the organization?
❑ Can you identify any spin-offs not directly related to the training objectives?
❑ Can we do a cost–benefit analysis to justify the investment?
❑ How will this experience affect future training decisions?

As with any set of managerial questions, you must involve the trainees themselves in answering them. Get the view also of anybody else who may have been involved: other managers, supervisors, training staff, Personnel.

If you can measure the amount of learning that has taken place, evaluation is comparatively easy. It becomes more difficult when competencies such as decision-making, problem-solving, creativity or presentation of ideas are involved. In these cases, you can consider evaluating the training in other ways.

Involve the trainee in evaluation. Ask for their immediate responses. Monitor those responses over time: they may come to feel differently about training after a period of reflection and implementation. If training is to improve performance, trainees must have the opportunity to practise their newly acquired skills as soon as possible. Training usually only lasts for a short time and skills development is necessarily a slower and more gradual process. When trainees return, ask them what they've learnt; ask how they intend to implement the training; give further opportunities through coaching, assignment, projects, job rotation or even secondment.

Take an interest in what trainees bring back from training events. You can vastly increase the value of your investment in training by asking them to transmit what they've learnt to the rest of the team – including you! Invite them to make presentations and to develop any materials they may have brought back into support documentation that everyone can use. All of this activity will help you evaluate the training itself, as well as monitoring each trainee's performance.

Keep a record of training. You might consider keeping individual records of all a person's learning experiences while working with you, and a departmental or team record summarizing all the team's training.

COACHING

Coaching is improving the performance of an already competent performer. Establishing a competency, perhaps, is training; developing a competency *in action* is coaching. It usually happens one-to-one, is an on-the-job activity and proceeds continuously.

Coaching is potentially one of the most rewarding of your activities as a manager. Most coaching is done by the more senior person but you don't have to be in a subordinate position to be coached. What is essential is that the coach should have the qualities of expertise, judgement and experience that allow the coachee to follow their guidance. (I rather dislike the word 'coachee', but it is useful. I'll continue to use it here in the absence of anything better.)

At the heart of coaching is a conversation. An effective coach helps the coachee think for themselves, fostering greater **awareness** and hence greater **responsibility**.

Fostering awareness is the first stage of coaching and involves what I call first-stage thinking: thinking about what we are looking at, what we can perceive. At this stage, we are using coaching to look at:

❑ what is going on;
❑ the goals;
❑ what we need to know;
❑ dynamics and relationships between the coachee and others;
❑ wider organizational issues;
❑ the coachee's own feelings; fears, emotions, desires, intuitions, capabilities.

Fostering responsibility is the second stage of coaching and involves second-stage thinking: thinking about what to do. So at this stage, coaching encourages the coachee to think about:

❑ ideas for action;
❑ opportunities for change or growth;
❑ deciding what to do and how to do it;
❑ taking action.

It will be clear that these two stages of thinking – and of coaching – relate closely to the four stages of the standard conversational structure I've used throughout the book. Fostering awareness relates to the welcoming and acquiring conversations: the conversations for relationship and possibility. Fostering responsibility relates to the supplying and parting conversations: the conversations for opportunity and action.

The essence of the coach's role is to ask questions. This point cannot be stressed too heavily. Instructing will tend to generate a minimal response: the action carried out, but little more. Asking a question focuses attention, increases awareness and encourages the coachee to take responsibility. To quote an old Chinese proverb:

What I hear I forget.
What I see I remember.
What I do I know.

Asking questions also helps the coach. Instead of forging ahead with a sequence of orders, the coach can use questions to follow the trains of thought, the interest, the enthusiasm or the emotional reactions of the coachee– and adapt the coaching accordingly.

Of course, it is essential for the coach to listen to the coachee's answers – and pick up on them. Coaching should be a genuine dialogue. The most effective questions are those that encourage the coachee to think independently. The coach's task is not to transfer expertise, nor to emphasize the coachee's accountability.

Questions that point up the coachee's ignorance or subservience are unhelpful.

The coach, then, should be careful to ask genuine questions: not rhetorical, sarcastic, facetious, loaded or leading questions. Ask questions that:

❑ indicate how well the coach understands a situation;
❑ suggest what to ask next;
❑ monitor the coachee's progress against an objective;
❑ promote responsibility in the coachee for a decision.

The best kinds of questions are open, non-judgemental and specific.

During first-stage thinking, when we are fostering clearer awareness, the coach should ask questions that require specific or quantifiable answers:

❑ 'What...?'
❑ 'Where...?'
❑ 'When...?'
❑ 'Who...?'
❑ 'How many...?'
❑ 'How much...?'

Avoid 'Why...?' and 'How...?' They will tend to imply judgement, analysis or criticism, which are all forms of second-stage thinking. If necessary, 'Why...?' can become 'What were the reasons for...' and 'How...?' might be better put as 'What were the steps that...?'

During second-stage thinking, the same kinds of questions can serve to focus on what the coachee will do next, how, when, where and so on.

The ladder of inference is a useful tool in this process. Walking the coachee down the ladder from beliefs or assumptions to specific observations will encourage a wider awareness; walking up the ladder through meanings, judgement and belief to action will strengthen motivation and a sense of responsibility for future actions.

Can a manager be a coach?

Is it possible for a line manager to fill the role of coach? How can we square the admirable aims of coaching with our other managerial roles?

The critical issue here is accountability. It may be difficult to engage in a genuine dialogue when the coachee is accountable to you for performance standards or meeting targets. Unless accountability is clearly recognized and acknowledged, it can become a demon overshadowing the entire coaching process. On the other hand, you may be in the best possible position to act as coach. You should know the coachee better than almost anybody else in the organization. And you are best placed to deal with these very issues of accountability. The best policy must be to clarify the standards, targets and key responsibilities for which the coachee is accountable to you. Indeed, coaching can provide an opportunity for the coachee to become more aware of the reasons for standards and targets, and therefore more responsible for meeting them.

Coaching is a delicate and sensitive process. It requires the very best qualities of any manager:

❑ keen listening and observation;
❑ integrity;
❑ detachment;
❑ supportiveness;
❑ interest;
❑ patience.

A good coach must be able to empathize with the coachee and yet retain a keen sense of self-awareness. Intuition and the ability to withhold judgement are vital. At its best, coaching challenges your own observation, values, assumptions, and beliefs as a manager. Coaching can be a good opportunity to re-examine your own awareness and sense of responsibility. It can become a dialogue that results in learning on both sides: a genuine partnership. Coaching can be the most rewarding part of your role as a manager.

The four stages of coaching

There are four parts to the coaching process. The traditional model for this is based on the word GROW:

❑ **GOAL-SETTING:** for the session and for the coachee's development;
❑ **REALITY** analysis, to explore the current situation for difficulties and opportunities;
❑ **OPTIONS** for future courses of action;
❑ **WHAT** to do: a 'hard' decision on action, WHEN and by WHOM.

It will be clear that these four stages relate closely to the four stages of the standard conversational structure I've used throughout the book. Fostering awareness (goal-setting and reality analysis) relates to the welcoming and acquiring conversations – the conversations for relationship and possibility. Fostering responsibility (options for action and what to do) relates to the supplying and parting conversations – the conversations for opportunity and action.

Goal-setting
The initial task is to decide the purpose of the coaching: to establish our goal, both for the coaching session itself and for the performance issue being coached.

First-stage thinking here is a matter of reviewing and proliferating goals. It's not enough simply to set a single goal; take time to

find the possibilities of others, or of looking at the first goal definition in different ways. Think of the coachee's goals as statements
beginning 'How to' and take a little time to generate as many new
'How to' statements as you can from the original goal. This helps
you both to explore the coachee's deeper values, their higher
aspirations and longer-term ambitions.

Now you can categorize these numerous 'how to' statements.
Some will be end goals; others will be performance goals, measurable levels of performance that may set you on the path to an end
goal or prove that you've achieved it. All of them are revealing,
but you will only be able to choose one or two for immediate
coaching. The best goals to choose, for practical purposes, are
those that generate the greatest creative tension between goal
and reality. Like the tension in a taut elastic band that stores
potential energy, it is creative tension that will provide the energy
for movement. Which goals excite the coachee most? Which generate the most commitment?

The choice of goal must be the coachee's. The goal should be
attainable – not beyond the coachee's capabilities or out of reach,
but also challenging enough to maintain the tension. The coach's
role is to help the coachee decide how attainable and challenging
the goal is, and review it in the wider context of the coachee's
work responsibilities and objectives.

Reality analysis
Creative tension depends as much on a clear perception of reality
as on a clear goal.

Look reality coolly in the face. Be objective; avoid judgement.
Instead of describing past performance, for example, as 'bad' or
'inadequate', focus on the specific aspects of it that need improvement. Walk the coachee down the ladder of inference and offer
verifiable, measurable observations:

❑ 'What have you tried so far?'
❑ 'What were the results?'
❑ 'Exactly how much under target did you come in?'

❑ 'What resources do you lack?'
❑ 'When did you last check the situation?'
❑ 'Where were the actual difficulties?'

Remember that a good deal of current reality is inner reality. Follow where the coachee's concerns take you and (gently) investigate their emotional responses:

❑ 'How did you feel when you tried...?'
❑ 'What emotions arise when you talk about...?'
❑ 'Is there anything you're afraid of?'
❑ 'How do you think you might be preventing yourself from achieving more?'
❑ 'How confident do you feel right now about achieving this goal?'

Virtually all of us have been programmed from a very early age with two deep-seated beliefs that inhibit our ability to pursue challenging goals:

❑ a sense of **powerlessness:** that we are incapable of achieving what we want;
❑ a sense of **unworthiness:** that, in some way, we don't deserve to succeed.

These beliefs – and there are few of us who have not experienced one or other of them – are part of the current reality of coaching. Surfacing them can help both coach and coachee to understand the deeper reasons for reluctance, hostility or concern about pursuing a goal. Facing our demons can help us to conquer them.

It is as well, however, to be cautious in this area: you are coaching, not counselling. If in doubt, leave alone. Assess which aspects of reality are most relevant to your goals.

Options for action
This is potentially the most creative part of the coaching process. Our purpose here is to find as many options for action as possible, in order to choose specific, realistic next steps. Once again, it is important to recognize that inner reality may be inhibiting the choice. The opponent within one's own head can be a powerful censor:

❑ 'It can't be done.'
❑ 'We can't do it like that.'
❑ 'They would never agree to it.'
❑ 'It will be too expensive.'
❑ 'Altogether too risky/disruptive/complicated/radical.'
❑ 'I don't have the time.'
❑ 'That's already been tried – and look what happened.'

You might counter these objections with 'what if' questions:

❑ 'What if we could do it?'
❑ 'What if this barrier didn't exist?'
❑ 'What if we could get them to agree?'
❑ 'What if we found a budget?'
❑ 'What if we managed the risk/minimized disruption/made it simpler...?'
❑ 'What if we reallocated resources?'
❑ 'What if we tried again?'

Keep your options open:

❑ 'What else could you do?'
❑ 'Could you do it differently?'
❑ 'Are there other ways of meeting this target or goal?'

Choosing an option is very much a second-stage thinking task. Carefully examine the costs and benefits of the action. Don't limit yourselves to one option: it may be possible to merge two or more as a realistic course of action, or schedule options as immediate and longer-term. Check that the chosen option is:

❑ attainable:
  – budgeted, costed, properly resourced;
  – specific and measurable;
  – realistic in wider organizational terms;
  – scheduled;
❑ challenging:
  – requiring new activity or research;
  – exciting to the coachee;
  – moving reality closer to the goal (and doesn't lower the goal!);
  – going to enhance or add skills;
  – going to improve performance;
  – going to be a genuine learning experience.

What to do
This part of the coaching process is about drawing up a detailed action plan:

❑ 'What are you going to do?'
❑ 'When will you do it?'
❑ 'Will this action (or series of actions) move you towards your goal?'
❑ 'What barriers might you have to overcome?'
❑ 'Who else will be involved?'
❑ 'What support do you need?'; 'Where will you find it?'
❑ 'What other consequences are there of this course of action, and how do we deal with them?'

And it is vital for the coach to ask:

❑ 'What can I do to help?'

This part of coaching requires a lot of hard-headed second-stage thinking if an action plan is going to be workable – and if the coachee is actually going to carry it through.

It is critically important, too, to establish issues of accountability, if only to clear them out of the way. How will the coachee be accountable to you in this plan? What targets shall we set? Might we need to review them? If so, when? Ideally, these accountable targets should be minimal and agreed between coach and coachee – as they would at an appraisal.

Document the agreed action plan, and sign it, to confirm that the coachee is committed to carrying it through. Build in a review date to monitor progress.

COUNSELLING

At some stage you will almost certainly have to help somebody through a difficult situation. This is the most obvious cause of a counselling conversation. But counselling skills are useful in other, less stressful situations as well. Counselling may come into play around issues like difficulties with colleagues or managers, career choices, or even significant changes in social or personal circumstances.

Counselling, like coaching, helps someone to help themselves. Unlike coaching, we are not helping to develop a competency, but helping to resolve a situation that the person sees as a problem.

Counselling is not giving advice. Part of the skill of management – we have seen this over and over again in this book – is the ability to help people find their own solutions. As a counsellor, your role is to provide a different perspective from which to try out ideas. The counselled person (I suppose we have for convenience to call them the 'counsellee'!) must find their own solution and exercise their own responsibility. Neither the counsellor nor the counsellee knows the answer at the start of the counselling conversation. The answer emerges from the conversation itself.

Counselling, more than any other managerial conversation, demands deep listening skills. Indeed, you may be required to do nothing but listen. You must be willing to believe that the counsellee has something to say; you must be sure to check that you have clearly understood it. You must give this conversation your undivided attention and as much time as it needs. It should go without saying that the conversation is private and completely free from interruption.

You may be working in an organization that offers professional counselling. But it's unlikely that you will be able to avoid this kind of conversation completely. Neither should you. Remember that you may not be a trained counsellor and that therefore your responsibility in this area should be limited by your managerial responsibilities.

Counselling always relies on the assumption that the counsellee has the skills, knowledge and – deep down – the desire to find a solution. It also assumes that these skills and qualities are impeded in some way. The impediment may be no more than the belief that they don't know what to do. They may be too close to the problem, or too immersed in emotion to be able to think rationally.

The counsellor's role is to help the counsellee step back and see it differently, so that they can find a new way forward.

Essential qualities of a good counsellor

Your style as a counsellor will be key to the success of the conversation. Counselling is not just about making somebody feel better; it is about achieving a new perception of a situation and a new approach to acting in it.

You must respect the counsellee. You must suspend judgement. Trust the good sense of the counsellee and believe that they will be able to arrive at a sensible decision and a sound plan of action. This may not be easy if you know them well.

You must also be able to retain the counsellee's trust. This is especially important for matters of confidentiality and to help you challenge apparent flaws or misperceptions in the counsellee's analysis. Retaining someone's trust and challenging their thinking is a difficult task. You may have to help the counsellee to face up to uncomfortable truths about themselves and their situation.

At the heart of this difficulty is the idea of empathy. This is best defined in contrast to sympathy. Sympathy is literally 'feeling with' the other person: you take on the emotion that they display. If they cry, you will probably cry too. Empathy is displaying an understanding of the emotions and feelings the counsellee displays *without* feeling them yourself – much more difficult to achieve. It is this sense of caring detachment that counselling – and the counsellee themselves – requires of you.

Empathy doesn't deny you the opportunity to talk (briefly) about similar experiences that you might have had in the problem area. It's important to distinguish this kind of understanding from the kind of examples you may be tempted to give of similar problems that you have helped others solve. Empathy is a matter of displaying an understanding of the problem without offering ready-made solutions. Equally important is the rule that you shouldn't descend into criticism of others. If you show that you can denigrate someone to another's face, the counsellee will almost certainly put two and two together and wonder whether you would criticize them in the same way.

The skills of counselling

The skills of counselling are not unlike the skills we use every day when people tell us about their problems. The difference is that you must behave professionally; in other words, honestly, consistently and without prejudice. Your contribution should be well informed and appropriate to the situation. Sadly, many day-to-day counselling conversations lack all of these qualities.

Beyond the essential skill of listening, there are three main skills that come to the fore in counselling:

❑ asking open questions;
❑ reflecting;
❑ confronting.

Used well, they will all help to make the conversation more productive.

Asking open questions
Open questions, by definition, cannot be answered 'Yes' or 'No'. They often include the words why, who, what, when, where and how. They are particularly useful in the early stages of the conversation. They can also give the other person some opportunity to contribute and influence the direction the discussion takes.

Reflecting
Counsellors use reflection in three main ways. They reflect:

❑ what people seem to be feeling;
❑ their words, the content of what they have said;
❑ the implied content.

Reflecting feelings. This is probably the first, and the most useful, technique likely to be used in a counselling session. It leads to greater clarity about the issue being discussed while helping the speaker to know that the listener really does understand. Frequently it needs to be no more than a few words:

❑ 'You feel angry.'
❑ 'You seem to be distracted.'
❑ 'Perhaps you are confused.'

It doesn't seem to matter if you are contradicted. If you suggest that the counsellee is angry, they can easily answer: 'No, I am disappointed...' and they will tell you why. (This may include an explanation of just why they are angry! All counsellors have had the experience of clients confirming later something they could not admit or face early on in a session.)

Reflecting the speaker's words. This is a very simple and effective technique, which enables you to prompt the counsellee without running the risk of the discussion going off track. It can open up issues, and help to break through a block. The counsellor listens carefully for emotionally charged words, those given undue emphasis, or for which the speaker's voice fades or becomes barely audible. Simply repeating one such word can help the counsellee to move on.

Reflecting content. The trick here is simply to repeat what the counsellee has just told you.

❏ 'You say that you are not being challenged enough.'

It usually results in an elaboration of the point that has been made and provides a way forward. Sometimes you can reflect something that has only been hinted at. Perhaps the counsellee can't quite bring themselves to say it, but they will talk volubly on the subject if you legitimize it for them. I remember once saying: 'You feel we are biased against females here'. I then sat in total silence for twenty minutes while all the other person's emotions – and a lot of very hard evidence – poured out.

The dangers with reflecting are that you may suggest something they do not feel, or give the impression that you think that your statement is true. It should only be used with great discretion and the words *you feel* are important.

Confronting
Use this technique with great care. It may consist simply of asking for concrete detail to support an allegation or an expression of vague feeling. It may involve pointing out apparent contradictions: between what the counsellee is saying and what he or she said earlier; between what is said and the way of saying it; between

words and body language. Remember that you are confronting perceptions in order to root out possible new ones. You are *not* confronting to criticize or to degrade the counsellee in any way.

The four stages of counselling

The four stages of counselling are very like those of coaching. The main difference between them is in emphasis. Coaching is about reaching a goal and improving in some way; counselling is essentially about removing some obstacle or difficulty and simply being able to move on.

Stage one: diagnosis
This is the conversation for relationship. You need to establish at the outset a positive relationship between counsellor and counsellee. The counsellee will almost certainly be feeling vulnerable and anything you can do to put them at their ease – to create the trust and respect that they need – is essential.

What is the problem as the counsellee sees it? Where is the blockage?

Stage two: exploration
This is the conversation for possibility. Some aspect of this problem is probably buried, because the counsellee either is unwilling to bring it to the surface (for fear of the consequences) or is not aware of it. Help them to step back and examine the possibilities of the situation:

❑ 'Why do you think you feel this way?'
❑ 'What kind of response do you think you might get if you told X about this?'
❑ 'Who else has contributed to the problem?'
❑ 'How do you think this has arisen?'
❑ 'What might be the cause of the problem?'

You might consider making the conversation more creative at this stage by asking the counsellee to think about the problem in radically different ways:

❑ 'What does this problem look like?'
❑ 'If you were the problem, how would you feel?'
❑ 'Can you think of another way of expressing the problem?'

In some situations, you may be able to help the counsellee to transform the problem in some radical way. The counsellee very often sees the problem as external; a burden to be borne or an obstacle to be overcome. A key stage in taking ownership of the problem is to see it instead as a goal for which the counsellee can take responsibility.

Invite the counsellee to try to frame the problem as a 'how to' statement. The idea is that, by doing so, the problem becomes expressed as an objective: a way forward that the counsellee might want to take. A 'how to' statement also implies multiple possibilities of movement: if you are asking 'how to' achieve a goal, the mind immediately responds with: 'well, you might...or you might...' and so on. Better still, you might help the counsellee to try several different 'how to' statements as a way of exploring different aspects of the problem. This can have the effect of lightening the conversation and helping the counsellee to gain some objectivity.

This transformation of an obstacle into a goal is at the very heart of the counselling process. You should approach it with care. A counsellee may all too easily feel pressure at this point to take ownership of a problem while lacking any desire to. You must use all your skill and sensitivity to manage this most crucial part of the process.

Stage three: opportunities
The conversation for opportunity should lead the counsellee to envisage possible courses of action and their consequences. The counsellee should be moving from emotion to a more considered attitude without any pressure from you. They should be visualizing

various results and the feelings these would evoke. The counsellee should now be feeling more enabled to choose a course of
action.

Stage four: action
In this conversation for action, you are not making a request –
beyond the simple request that the counsellee makes a decision.
Now that they can see the situation more clearly and has assessed
various options, there is a need to make a move. It might be a very
small one; it might be the beginnings of a planned strategy.
(Many of my own more stressful problems seem to dissolve in the
face of a clear plan.)

   If you have helped someone to make a clear plan, then your
counselling has succeeded. You both need to feel that you have
anticipated most of the likely outcomes of the proposed action
and that, between you, you have the resources to cope with them.
You can also use this stage of the conversation to help the
counsellee reflect on the skills, knowledge, experience and personal qualities that are likely to help in resolving the problem.

6

MANAGING A TEAM

This is the age of the team. Many a manager these days will see themselves as a team leader, as well as a member of one or more teams of their peers. In many organizations, what used to be called 'departments' are now renamed 'teams'; if you are working in a project-based environment, teams will be the basic working units. You will not survive as a manager, the received wisdom tells us, without teamworking skills.

The idea of teams has been growing since at least the 1960s, when John Adair and John Garnett introduced the powerful concept of team briefing. The notion has survived too long to be considered a fad or gimmick. Teams are here to stay. The organization of the future looks like being flatter than the organization of the past, with fewer layers of management. Its success will depend more upon the exchange of information, and on people's ability to solve problems together, than on the supply of raw materials or labour. For these reasons, if for no others, the manager of the future will have to be a team player.

Not everybody, though, shares the uncritical adulation that teamwork often receives. Research by one consultancy firm, quoted in *The Economist* on 14 January 1995, found that nearly 7 out of 10 teams don't produce expected results. This failure may be partly because teams are not always well managed, and partly because teams are more difficult to manage than other kinds of groupings. Teams can perform brilliantly but they also require a lot of maintenance and this can make them costly. Teams may also be failing because managers are not being trained sufficiently in the dynamics of teams – or because they are spending too much effort on team-building at the expense of the work to be done.

Above all, I think that teams are overused. Teams are not a panacea for all ills. Much – probably most – of what we do at work does not need to be done by a team. It needs to be done by individuals, exercising their action responsibilities. To introduce teamwork for this kind of work can be irrelevant or positively harmful. On the other hand, there is probably a small part of what we do where teamwork is essential, and to ignore the need for it is inviting disaster. Part of your responsibility as a manager is to distinguish clearly where teamwork is needed and where it may actually stop people from doing their work properly.

Organizations sometimes apply teamwork unthinkingly where other kinds of solution may be more appropriate: radical leadership, a change of technology or entrepreneurial individualism. As a manager within a larger organizational structure and culture, you need to think about how teams have been introduced and what problems may have arisen with operating them.

PROBLEMS WITH TEAMS: MANAGEMENT

❑ introduced to compensate for weak strategy;
❑ used as cover for poor business practice;
❑ placed within a hostile organizational culture (command and control; individual reward systems; resistance from middle management);
❑ a lack of long-term commitment;
❑ lessons from one team not transferred to others;
❑ poor objectives set: vague or conflicting assignments;
❑ inadequate training;
❑ inappropriate membership;
❑ a lack of trust.

All of these problems can produce difficulties within teams themselves. People become disillusioned and frustrated. Teamwork acquires a bad reputation and becomes something of a bad joke.

PROBLEMS WITH TEAMS: TEAM MEMBERS

❏ trying to achieve too much too early;
❏ clashes of work style or individual approach;
❏ results emphasized at the expense of group dynamics;
❏ encountering unforeseen obstacles;
❏ resistance to a new approach;
❏ poor interpersonal skills;
❏ a lack of team culture.

Teams can never magically replace the need for clear areas of responsibility and lines of accountability. If you are in charge of a team, you need to be clear about:

❏ why teamwork is promoted in your organization;
❏ what you and your team mean by the word 'team';
❏ where teamwork is helpful and where it may hinder your operation;
❏ what team members expect from the team;
❏ how groups of people behave;
❏ how to organize and lead your team for maximum effectiveness.

WHY TEAMWORK?

A team is somewhere to call home. I believe that this, more than anything else, explains the huge popularity of teams in large organizations. Teams may not be necessary for most kinds of work, but they do provide a way to satisfy people's social needs.

We can use Maslow's hierarchy of needs to see how teams achieve this. A team sounds more welcoming than a department, so it provides a place of safety. A team is a small number of people who feel that they belong together, so it can satisfy our need for respect and affection. A team is small enough for people's contribution to be noticed, so it can provide a forum for us to establish a reputation and gain recognition from others. It's easier to notice achievement in a team and easier to praise it. And, because a team protects its members to some extent from the responsibilities and risks of the organization as a whole, it is a context for self-fulfilment. We can experiment, try things out, develop and test new skills within the safe confines of the team.

We can translate these benefits into work benefits. Because teams can satisfy people's social needs, they can help people to release their energy for more productive and energetic work. And because teams are locally managed units, they can also help people to understand better what they are supposed to be doing and how. As a result, teams are said to create:

❑ less stress;
❑ a greater understanding of the job role;
❑ a deeper sense of contribution to the organization;
❑ increased productivity;
❑ increased job satisfaction;
❑ closer control;
❑ a forum for development;
❑ more open communication;
❑ a place to exercise the corporate values of the organization.

So a team is not only 'home', but also a mediator between the individual and the organization. The organization can come alive for people within the context of the team.

You must pay attention to the social aspects of your team. We all have a certain amount of energy available to give to our work.

We use some of that energy to meet the needs Maslow describes. Whatever is left we can devote to our work. In theory, a team allows us to satisfy those needs with a minimum of energy, leaving lots of energy left for our work! In a failing team, people need to use up more and more energy for emotional survival – to avoid getting hurt or to protect their sense of self-esteem. The result will be loss of productivity and poor quality.

A team that fails to address people's social needs will fail as a work unit. That's why so much attention is paid to the chemistry of teams, to assembling dream teams made up of just the right mix of people. Many consultancies offer models and processes and analytical tools to help teams profile themselves. Most of us, in reality, are limited in our ability to alter a team's profile. We aren't able to build a team from scratch; we have to work with the people we've got. The important thing is to recognize the social needs of your team and to seek to address them – principally through conversations of various kinds.

People join teams to satisfy their own individual needs. But teams, like all groups of people, have a life of their own. To understand how to manage a team, it's useful to begin with examining how groups behave.

Knowing how people behave in groups will allow us to:

❑ understand better what is actually going on in the team;
❑ appreciate why team conversations differ from conversations between individuals;
❑ anticipate conflict and prevent or tackle it;
❑ manage the team's behaviour;
❑ improve the team's output or results.

So we must examine how groups develop; the structures within groups that emerge from that process; and how those structures encourage or discourage certain kinds of behaviour.

HOW GROUPS WORK

We can define a group as any number of people who:

❑ interact with each other in some way;
❑ are aware of each other;
❑ perceive themselves to be a group.

This distinguishes groups from crowds or collections of individuals. A group, by our definition, is limited in numbers to about 12: any larger group will have difficulty in evolving a single identity, although subgroups will emerge. We can also distinguish between groups and teams, which are specific kinds of groups working together to achieve common objectives. Whether or not they see themselves as a team, people working together will certainly behave as members of a group.

Groups have two kinds of objectives:

❑ task objectives;
❑ social objectives.

Task objectives concern the job to be done and may be imposed or dictated from outside the group. Social objectives concern the group's developing sense of identity, its well-being and the relationships of group members to each other and to the group. They usually develop from within the group. All working groups will pursue both kinds of objectives. Problems arise particularly when:

❑ task objectives are obscured by social objectives (the group is having too much of a good time);
❑ task objectives suppress or damage social objectives (tasks imposed dictatorially, for example, or when the group is under stress);
❑ the two kinds of objectives come into conflict (for example, one part of the group seeking to impose tasks on another).

Groups can be formal or informal. Formal groups are consciously created by organizations to accomplish particular tasks or fulfil specific functions. Teams are formal groups. They may be permanent or temporary: administrative teams or project teams, for example. Informal teams emerge spontaneously from the interaction of individuals as they associate with each other, talking, joking, exchanging experiences and enjoying each other's company.

Both kinds of group exist in organizations. Informal groups, broadly speaking, satisfy the human needs that formal groups neglect or ignore. The more formal the group, the more task-oriented it will be; the more informal, the more socially oriented.

Many experts agree that, the more cohesive a group, the more productive it is. A group's cohesion emerges from mutually positive attitudes among group members, and is expressed in terms of both task and social objectives. If both task and social objectives are weak, the group's cohesion will be poor and its performance will certainly suffer. Strong task objectives and poor social objectives may be somewhat effective: the group may get things done in a 'bad atmosphere', though at the cost of anxiety, stress, antagonism, frustration and hurt feelings. Achieving task objectives, of course, can strengthen social cohesion.

On the other hand, strong social objectives without a clear focus on task objectives can be just as damaging. A group where everybody is only 'bonding' or basking in self-congratulation will not be highly productive.

Clarifying task objectives is fundamental to any group's success. However, we ignore social objectives at our peril.

Group development

A group is made up of individuals. Once introduced into a group, our primary desire is to integrate with it. We pursue the aims of:

❑ well-being (physical, mental, emotional, economic, spiritual);
❑ a sense of belonging;

❑ recognition from the group;
❑ control over our own lives.

If the group satisfies these needs, we will respond by strengthening it. If we doubt that the group will satisfy them, we may hang back from full participation. If we become convinced that it cannot or will not support us, we will withdraw – physically or mentally – or pursue some other strategy. We may seek to create a subgroup or threaten the group's identity by engaging in sabotage. The group itself, meanwhile, begins to take on a life of its own. Its primary objective is to survive. If counteracting forces become too strong and the group splinters, new groups will start to form at once.

Groups affect individuals' behaviour; in turn, we can influence the groups we join. It is the complicated web of relationships within the group that is important.

Groups develop continually. A group may form, grow and destroy itself in a matter of hours; another may be stuck at one stage for months or even years. Barry Tuckman's four-stage model of a group's evolution, from inception to full maturity, has proved highly influential. It was developed in the mid-1960s and Tuckman was careful to point out that it was based on work with therapy sessions rather than working groups. Nonetheless, it has been repeated so often that many have come to see it as a standard model for group development; indeed, partly because of its easy labels and its appeal to common sense, it remains a powerful structure. And it seems to be borne out by experience.

Tuckman's model sees a group develop through four stages:

❑ forming;
❑ storming;
❑ norming;
❑ performing.

In 1977, he added a fifth stage – less often quoted – which he called 'adjourning'.

Forming
At the first stage, individuals have not yet become a group and are in a tentative relationship to each other. They are finding out about each other: their attitudes, background and values. They are also keen to establish their own identities and make an impression. It is a time of some anxiety and potential embarrassment. The group leader must strengthen the group quickly, by identifying what binds it together and by stating the rules governing its behaviour.

Storming
This stage is characterized by conflict. Group members challenge each other's versions of reality: what we can agree to be true, and where we differ. Value systems (what we regard as important or acceptable) and belief systems (the truths we hold to be self-evident) are thrashed out. At a dinner party, this conflict is the 'politics and religion' stage, which can be uncomfortable; at work, versions of reality may be disguised in terms of action: goals and preferred methods of working.

Relationships established in the forming stage may be disrupted or destroyed. Individuals will try tactical manoeuvres: seeking allies, withdrawing ('wait and see'), empire-building, vetoing, threatening to disrupt the proceedings, demanding the right to be recognized, resisting an onslaught against them. The group will try to resolve this conflict by agreeing a version of reality: the value and belief systems to which everybody can sign up.

Norming
The group has found a shared frame of reference: an agreed version of reality based on common perceptions, values and beliefs. These are the group's norms. It now develops a way of working to achieve its goals, allocating roles and rules of conduct: a practical framework in which people can work together. It is at this stage that *groupthink* can emerge.

Groupthink values the group above anything else. The word was first coined by Irving Janis. He looked into the US government's foreign policy fiascos in Vietnam and elsewhere. He concluded that foreign policy advisors had become so cohesive as a group that they were able to ignore obvious warning signs and make disastrous decisions. Janis defined groupthink as: 'a mode of thinking that people engage in when they are deeply involved in a cohesive group, when members' strivings for unanimity override their motivation to realistically appraise alternative courses of action.'

Groupthink is one of the greatest dangers to effective teamwork. It can arise in any situation where a team is operating without external checking mechanisms, or in an organization with a strong internal culture. People suffering from groupthink are friendly, tightly knit, and unlikely to disagree with each other. They will probably engage in private language and crack private jokes. Anybody who refuses to accept the team norms may be labelled as deviant or subversive. The group will apply increasingly painful pressure on them to conform.

Performing
The group gets on with the job in hand. It is fully mature. Not all groups develop this far. Many groups become stuck in an early stage – sometimes irretrievably. Others bounce back and forth between stages, or revert to an earlier stage with a change of membership.

Adjourning
The group's work is done and it is time to move on to other tasks and responsibilities. Many group members, having worked so hard to get along with each other and achieve the task, feel a keen sense of loss at this stage. As a result, some have called this stage 'mourning'. The return to independent life is often eased by rituals of one kind or another: awards ceremonies, parties or mock funerals provide a sense of punctuation at the end of a project. At this stage, the group leader must emphasize the valuable lessons

learnt from the group's experience, to prepare people for their next task and their next group effort.

Tuckman's model can help us in two ways. We can use it to help our team improve its performance, and it can indicate why a team may be underperforming. A group cannot evolve healthily from one stage to the next if issues in the earlier stage remain unresolved. Team leaders may try to reach the performing stage without having agreed a frame of reference in the norming stage. Teams may suffer at the norming stage because common values and goals have been left unclear. Team members may continue to manipulate the group to achieve personal, 'political' goals, dragging it back into storming, or even destroying it completely so that forming must start anew.

Group structure

As the group evolves through these four stages, it develops a structure. We seek predictability in a group: uncertainty about others' behaviour is threatening. The group's structure protects it from this threat of unpredictable behaviour.

Group structure is neither fixed nor permanent. It is a complex, dynamic system, operating along a number of dimensions, including:

❑ status;
❑ power;
❑ role;
❑ leadership;
❑ liking.

We can interpret people's behaviour in a team as evidence of their efforts to find their place in the group structure, to move within it or to challenge it.

Status

Each position in the group has a value assigned to it. This status may arise formally or socially. Formal status is the collection of rights and duties associated with a position. Social status is the rank of a person as measured by the group – the degree of respect the group gives to that person.

A group confers status on anybody who meets the group's expectations. We may seek status within a group to meet our need for a sense of belonging, recognition from the group or well-being. Our status in a group is always at risk. It is created entirely through others' perceptions (we may call it 'good name' or 'reputation'). It can be destroyed or diminished in a moment. Downgrading a person's status in the group can be a powerful way of exerting the group's authority.

Power

Power is the control we can exert over others. If we can influence or control people's behaviour in any way, we have power over them. John French and Bertram Raven, in the late 1950s, identified five kinds of power base:

❑ reward power: the ability to grant favours for behaviour;
❑ coercive power: the ability to punish others;
❑ legitimate power: conferred by law or other sets of rules;
❑ referent power: the 'charisma' that causes others to imitate or idolize;
❑ expert power: deriving from specific levels of knowledge or skill.

French and Raven suggest that the broader the base of power, the more influential a person can be. Referent power is especially effective. We all know how influential charisma can be, even when we cannot define it.

People may seek to exercise different kinds of power at different times. A team member with little reward power may seize an opportunity to influence the team as an expert; a team leader lacking charisma or respect may try to exert authority by appealing to legitimate or to coercive power.

Role
Our role in the group is the set of behaviours expected of us by the group. Charles Handy has suggested that, when we join a group, we ask three questions.

1. **What is my identity in the group?** What is my task role? What do people expect me to do?
2. **Where is power located in the group?** Who has it? What kind is it? Do I want to exert power of any kind?
3. **What are my objectives?** What do I need? Are they in line with those of the group? What will I do if they are not?

Our answers to these questions will guide us towards the roles we play in the group.

Meredith Belbin's model of task roles is probably the most famous. Thousands of managers have now used Belbin's questionnaire to locate themselves among his categories of:

❑ chair/coordinator;
❑ shaper/team leader;
❑ plant/innovator or creative thinker;
❑ monitor-evaluator/critical thinker;
❑ company worker/implementer;
❑ team worker/team-builder;
❑ finisher/detail-checker and pusher;
❑ resource investigator/researcher outside the team.

Recently, Belbin has felt the need to add a further role, that of expert. A successful team, according to Belbin, will contain a balance of all nine roles; a team too strong in any one or more will perform less successfully.

Social roles have been investigated in numerous ways. We may recognize a few traditional social roles in groups: the mediator, the devil's advocate, the licensed fool. A well-established technique distinguishes between aggressive, passive and assertive behaviour. This simple model identifies different social roles in a group in terms of the way we exercise our strength with others. Other models are more complex. Transactional analysis, for example, identifies relationships between 'parents', 'children' and 'adults'. Neuro-linguistic programming (NLP) breaks down role-playing into even more elements.

Leadership
This dimension of group structure is closely related to all the others, even if a leader is imposed on the group from outside. We can define leadership in this context as behaviour that helps the group to achieve its preferred objectives. Leadership is now often referred to as a 'facilitative' activity: doing whatever *allows* the group to achieve, rather than directing people's energy in certain directions. It's useful, too, to distinguish between task leadership and process leadership. The first focuses on the job to be done, the second on building good relations within the group.

Liking
The liking dimension emerges spontaneously, helping people to gain status or power, or allowing them to exercise effective leadership.

The simple distinction between liking and disliking seems crude. We can find others attractive in many different ways or take against them in ways we may not be able – or willing – to articulate. Liking can become an emotional entanglement or even a fully-fledged relationship; dislike can turn into a vendetta or a curious, half-coded game of tit-for-tat. We may be unaware of the structures of like and dislike in the group, and may have to rely on clues. Our own behaviour may be adversely influenced, too, by anecdotal evidence given us by members of the group – evidence we may sometimes wish we had not been given!

Group authority

A group uses its structure to exercise authority over its members. Norms are the group's identifying features. To resist or violate them puts group cohesion at risk. At the norming stage, therefore, the group will exert pressure to conform on anybody whom it perceives to be deviating from them. Group members may be:

❑ encouraged: by humour, gentle sarcasm, pointed remarks;
❑ embarrassed: categorized as weak, stupid, irresponsible, odd – even evil;
❑ excluded: temporarily but deliberately left out of the conversation;
❑ expelled: told to 'shut up or get out'.

Whenever we see a group behaving towards an individual in any of these ways, we know that certain norms have been established.

The pressure to conform to group norms can be enormous. It can prevent us from contributing ideas, or dictate what ideas we should have – and even determine how we perceive reality. This pressure can easily overwhelm the authority of a delegated leader, removing all effective power or status, no matter how influential they may seem to be.

We can respond to this pressure in one of three ways; we can:

❑ argue our case, fight our corner and try to persuade others to join us;
❑ conform and suppress any opinion or behaviour that offends the group;
❑ withdraw ('There is a world elsewhere', to quote from Shakespeare's *Coriolanus*).

What we do will depend on our location in the group structure. If we have a great deal of power, we may easily persuade the group to change its norms in our favour. If we have high status or are much liked, the group may tolerate deviant behaviour rather than lose a valuable member.

So much for groups. Teams, as we have said, are specific kinds of groups and they must be treated in special ways. But everything that applies to groups applies equally to teams. Indeed, these models of group development and behaviour will help us now to see teams a lot more clearly – and then manage them more effectively.

DEFINING A TEAM

Here is a definition of a team. Let's examine it and see how well it stands up.

A team is a group of people working together to achieve common objectives.

At once we can see that the word 'team' actually encompasses *two* kinds of group. One we might call a 'work group' and the other a 'team'. These two broad definitions grow out of the history of the word itself – a history full of interesting twists and turns.

The word 'team' is very old. Its original meaning is 'childbearing': from the start the word has associations of fertility and giving life. We've entirely lost this meaning in modern English, although we can still hear a faint echo of it when we use the words 'teem' or 'teeming', meaning to be full of life. Later a 'team' came to mean a brood of animals, particularly geese or pigs. Thence it came to describe a group of animals working together: a team of horses ploughing, for example. This is where the idea of work first appears in connection with the word. By the seventeenth century, this meaning had become applied as well to people. A team of workmen were 'harnessed' together to pull in one direction, under the direction of a leader or foreman.

At about the same time, the word came to apply to a group of people playing as one side in a game. A football team, for example, is a group of people working towards a common objective. But this new meaning is subtly different from the first. A football team is not in harness: each player has a great deal of individual freedom of movement, which the team must coordinate in complex ways to achieve their goal (interesting that we use this word at work as well as in football!). A football team differs in other ways from the harnessed team, too. The team members are specialists: without a range of skills, the team would be impoverished and unsuccessful. They follow a broad strategy rather than a rigidly imposed process. Interestingly, they are also engaged in a performance task that has a defined time limit.

Two kinds of team

So we now have two complementary definitions of teams.

❑   functional teams (or work groups);
❑   creative teams.

In a *functional* team, a group of people performs a function that is a part of some larger process. The work is continuous and everybody in the team is doing essentially the same kind of work. They are equals under the guidance of a single team leader. Probably the majority of teams at work are of this kind: a team in a call centre, an administrative team, a cell on an assembly line. In the old days, functional teams might have been called departments. A finance department, a sales department, a housing department: all are functional teams.

In a *creative* team, a group of people with diverse skills are brought together to create a single result. Their work is not functional, not part of a larger operation; it is the whole task. A football team, for example, exists to create a winning game. But there are many other obvious examples of people operating as creative teams. A hospital team, for example, is drawn together to apply diverse skills to create a cured patient; a theatre company is a creative team drawn together to create a single production; a product team is a multi-functional team assembled to create a new product.

FUNCTIONAL TEAMS: TYPES AND EXAMPLES

Advice teams

❑ committees;
❑ review panels;
❑ quality circles;
❑ employee involvement groups;
❑ advisory councils.

Production teams

❑ assembly teams;
❑ manufacturing crews;
❑ mining teams;
❑ flight attendant crews;
❑ data processing groups;
❑ maintenance teams.

CREATIVE TEAMS: TYPES AND EXAMPLES

Project teams

❑ research groups;
❑ planning teams;
❑ architect teams;
❑ product teams;
❑ task forces.

Action teams

❑ sports teams;
❑ hospital teams;
❑ theatre groups;
❑ orchestras;
❑ expeditions;
❑ negotiating teams.

This simple distinction is very useful in helping you see more clearly what kind of team you are leading. Some would say that functional teams aren't strictly teams at all, but work groups. They might argue that the qualities of true teamwork only come into play when the work demands that a group of varied specialists comes together to create a single identifiable outcome. Certainly, the needs of functional and creative teams differ. In functional teams, the *social* aspects of the team come to the fore, because the work itself doesn't demand that people are organized as a team. In a creative team, the social needs remain important but the *task* aspects become more important. In a functional team, people will be more concerned to feel 'at home'; in a creative team, the focus will be very much on achieving the task.

How big should a team be?

Presumably, the smallest possible size of team is two people (a husband-and-wife team or a bobsleigh team). There are some psychologists who speak about the teamwork that exists within the sub-personalities of a single individual, but we are managers and not psychologists.

As for the upper limit, sport can provide some more useful ideas. Rugby Union, for example, has teams of fifteen, which sounds a good working maximum. In the context of a managerial span of control, it makes sense to think of a team as consisting of no more than about eight 'direct reports'. It certainly seems that a group much larger than this cannot hold effective meetings without some element of imposed control.

If your team is larger, ask how it can be seen as sub-units and how you can manage those units more effectively. It may be that the functional and creative aspects of your team's work will give you some help here. A fairly large team of social workers, for example, will usually break down into smaller casework teams on a regular basis.

Working towards common objectives

Another frequent cause of team failure is an unclear under-standing of objectives. Management may fail to set objectives, or set goals that the team find unrealistic. You must make sure that the team's objectives are explicit and that the team understands them. Ideally, of course, they will be involved in setting them as well.

You can think of team objectives in three ways:

❑ **Functional objectives.** These are the day-to-day objectives, the objectives that help the team to function. A sports team would address functional objectives through regular training. A management team would understand functional objectives in terms of planning, budgeting or the objectives cascaded down to it from higher levels of the organization.

❑ **Task objectives.** These are temporary, complete tasks. The sport's team's task objectives are to achieve winning games or high ranking; the orchestra's task objective is to play a certain piece of music to the best of its ability; an expedition's task objective is to reach its destination. Functional teams can find it hard to identify task objectives, because they don't exist to perform complete tasks. But a team culture – 'team spirit' and the high degrees of commitment and energy that we value in teams – can only arise through a focus on complete pieces of work. Very few of us can get excited about housekeeping chores.

❑ **Team objectives.** These are objectives relating to the well-being of the team itself. They will be expressed in terms of the team's values and what the team intends to contribute to the satisfaction of its members' needs. A team may make explicit its commitment to help team members develop their skills, to develop certain behaviours and attitudes, and to promote itself within the wider organization.

All of these objectives must be clearly understood, regularly reviewed and acted on – by the whole team. They form the basis of the contract that each team member makes in signing up to the team.

Generating commitment

Each member of the team must make the commitment to abide by the contract that they enter on joining the team.

In reality, of course, people's level of commitment will vary. After all, we may join a team simply because we want a job, or because we have been told to. We may see membership of the team as a milestone on our career path. People can also join teams with great enthusiasm, only to see their energy drained by incompetence or poor relationships within the team. A cynic is usually a passionate believer who has become disillusioned; they are potentially much more damaging to the team than a disinterested loner.

It is this contract between the individual and the team that defines the quality of the team's culture. Whether functional or creative, a team exists, for individual team members, to satisfy their *personal* needs. The better the balance between individual and team objectives, the more cohesive and successful the team will be, and the more satisfied the team members.

In making this contract, team members indicate that they are willing to sacrifice some element of personal autonomy to the team. They offer to make this sacrifice, *to the extent necessary to achieve common objectives*. Excessive constraints on personal autonomy will tend to create 'groupthink' among those who sign up, and resentment among those who have mentally resigned.

WHERE IS BRYSON?

I spent some time recently in Saudi Arabia, working with a group of managers for an electronics firm. They lived a life they saw as besieged, in an alien culture that forbade many social pleasures. So they turned in on themselves and took their pleasures privately. This reinforced the sense of team solidarity to such an extent that, if one member was absent at any of the innumerable team barbecues, the team leader would post messages on a white board in the lobby of the company villa. One night, I read: 'Where is Bryson? And why has Bryson not told us where he is going?'

I wondered whether attendance at barbecues was part of the contract Bryson had signed, and whether any other parts of his private life were under attack. Unfortunately, Bryson never turned up to tell me.

As the team leader, you have a special responsibility to maintain this balance between personal autonomy and responsibility to the team. You must find solutions that strengthen the team while allowing individuals to make the decisions that matter to them. This may mean trading one off against the other, or finding some third solution that works better than the team solution or the individual solution in respecting everybody's rights. In a crisis, it can be difficult for individuals to stand up against a team and refuse to work anti-social hours, for example. But, if the resistance is there, it will go underground and fester as a problem for another day.

You, the team leader, must decide whether the team is exploiting individuals or whether individuals are flouting their responsibilities to the team. You need to establish how far the team can constrain individual autonomy while maintaining the full commitment of the whole team. Through problem solving and negotiation, you need to formulate an explicit set of general rules to be observed by all team members. You also need to create individual 'contracts' that cover each team member's action responsibilities. It can be a tough responsibility to carry; you will carry it best, as ever, through the medium of conversation: with individuals, and with the team as a whole.

AUTONOMOUS TEAMWORK

What makes for an effective team? Everything we've looked at so far emphasizes the need for the team to have a clear identity, a clear sense of purpose and clear objectives. If you know *why* the team exists, what *kind* of team it is and what you want to *achieve*, you are well on the way to creating a team that will be effective.

What more does such a team need? Well, all the team members will be enthusiastic and committed; they will all be willing to get involved and participate. They will focus on achieving goals that are demanding and stretching, supporting each other and helping each other to develop skills and strengths. Members of an effective team will resist 'groupthink'. They will respect difference; they will be able to challenge each other honestly and openly; they will feel happy to challenge each other's views in the search for a better decision. The emphasis will be on growth and change as healthy and necessary. The rah-rah factor will be kept firmly under control.

I believe that any team's effectiveness depends entirely on the degree of respect the group gives to personal autonomy. People will commit freely to what they have chosen to do. They must be able to take ownership of their work. This means:

❑ having a clear sense of responsibility for the work;
❑ being emotionally committed to it; not doing the work merely because they have been told to or to earn a living.

The idea of autonomous teamwork grows out of the idea, explored earlier in this book, of action responsibility. It begins with a respect for the individual, rather than a desire to weld individuals into a team unit.

Actually, I don't think that this respect for personal autonomy need come into prolonged conflict with team identity. Most individuals want to make their contribution. They want to work with others and to be helpful. They look for support and for a sense of belonging. There is no reason why individual objectives and team objectives should not complement each other.

Action responsibility, as we have seen, defines what you do, and what you are responsible for doing. It defines your autonomy, the limits of your power as an individual. From the team's point of view, action responsibility demands a policy of 'Mind Your Own Business'. Team members should be able to do their work in their own way, without advice, help, ideas, criticism or opinions from their colleagues, unless they ask for such help, advice or opinions. Too often, team members, in their eagerness to be helpful, insist on imposing their ideas, opinions and solutions on colleagues who are quite capable of making their own decisions. This wastes time and can be destructive: one person's help is the other's interference. The Mind Your Own Business rule can also be stated as 'Offer ideas only when they are asked for.'

This doesn't mean that the team can't handle unsolicited ideas. On the contrary. The Mind Your Own Business rule demands that the team has a procedure for dealing with such ideas. You might set up a contractual arrangement so that, whenever an unsolicited idea emerges, the recipient is free to decide whether to accept the idea or discuss it. They are under no obligation to acknowledge or even comment on it. You might also hold regular brainstorming sessions to gather unsolicited ideas openly and manage them as a team.

The Mind Your Own Business rule extends to the limits of any one individual's action responsibility. It stops operating at any point when any individual's work impacts directly on another's area of responsibility. Any team is likely to have many such points of interaction. So you also need a set of conversations within the team to manage these points of shared responsibility.

TEAM CONVERSATIONS

There are four major team conversations. We can map them quite easily onto the four conversations we have already defined:

- ❑ **Relationship**. A conversation to agree objectives, strategies and values.
- ❑ **Possibility**. A conversation in which individuals seek help for a problem.
- ❑ **Opportunity**. An interactive problem-solving conversation.
- ❑ **Action**. Day-to-day supportive conversations.

Objectives, strategies and values

Every team needs to meet periodically – once a month, quarterly, or at least annually – to clarify its objectives and review its progress, and to remind itself what kind of team it wants to be. These 'team days' are critically important, particularly if they are infrequent. At their best, they renew the team's cohesion and give people the opportunity to sort out team problems. They put the team on a sound footing for the next period of operation.

Everybody on the team should regard team days as sacrosanct. Dates should be fixed well in advance. Nothing – but *nothing* – should displace them from the diary. The realities of modern business life can make it extremely difficult to keep team days clear. People will find it much easier to make this commitment if the organization as a whole commits to the idea. If the whole organization – or at least large sections of it – closes down once a quarter for a team day, its importance will be re-emphasized.

These high-profile meetings require a lot of planning. Usually the responsibility will be yours as the team leader, but you can delegate all or part of the task on occasions to another team member. You might consider also bringing in an external facilitator sometimes; a guest speaker or session leader. Using an outsider frees you from process responsibilities and allows you to join your team as a team member, concentrating on the issues being discussed.

Check with all team members what they would like included in the day. Focus on strategic issues: the team's mission or purpose, its values and where they might be being flouted, its operating procedures and where they might be strengthened.

The real purpose of these days is to strengthen the team. Shared objectives and values define a team. Agreeing them must therefore be a participatory process. Consensus is the best way to achieve the agreement you are seeking; try to avoid resorting to taking votes. The ultimate decisions must be yours, as team leader. You can create consensus by making the executive decision: people look to you to take the lead and will follow by consensus if they are convinced that it makes sense. They may not agree with your decision, but if you have acted as a responsible leader they will be happy to accept it. You should seek broad support for strategy without looking for unanimity on every small step. You should always make the reasons for your decision clear.

This important meeting is fundamentally a conversation for relationship. Who are we? Who are we to each other? Where do we stand? Where are we looking to go? Think about how the key principles of a conversation for relationship can expand to inform a team day.

Individual problem solving

This is a conversation for possibility. Like all such conversations, it can be a difficult conversation to hold. Individual team members may not find it easy to ask for help. In many organizations the stated ethos is that we are paid to solve our own problems and not inflict them on others. In such an atmosphere, to ask for help is virtually to confess to one's own inadequacy.

You as the team leader must therefore explicitly encourage these conversations to happen. You must make it clear that such conversations demonstrate the open-mindedness and willingness to learn that are fundamental values of any successful team. If, in addition, you are operating the Mind Your Own Business rule, it should become more natural for people to ask for help. The rule explicitly forbids people from offering unsolicited ideas; by the same token, it should encourage people to ask for help.

The style of this conversation should be one of offering help but not a solution (except in very simple situations). Team members need to become aware of the dynamics of a conversation for possibility, and of the questions and techniques it involves. In essence, the helper is striving to understand the problem as their colleague sees it, and assist the questioner to find his or her own solution.

Interactive problem-solving

This is a conversation for opportunity. The opportunities are usually signalled by argument or debate of some kind. The conflict is a sign that something is at stake: it may be an important team value or a strategy for moving forward. If you cannot resolve the conflict into a team problem to be solved, it's probably not worth continuing.

This conversation is principally about turning a conflict into an opportunity for action. By framing the problem as a 'how to', you open up the possibilities for creativity in examining and tackling it. Are you looking at a problem that needs some open, radical thinking, or a problem that can be sorted out by clear-headed planning? Where's the opportunity for growth, for development, for new successes?

Day-to-day support

I've classed these as action conversations, more for neatness than anything else. It is perhaps stretching the point a little to see these supportive conversations as formal requests for action in the way we have looked at conversations for action so far. But a conversation for action is itself an example of the kind of supportive conversation that underpins the life of any effective team. It rests on a sense of mutual respect and trust, an understanding that any request we make of our colleagues is for them to accept or reject. Nothing is taken for granted.

The close sharing between colleagues in an effective team runs on an emotional level as well as on a functional or task level. Individuals' successes contribute to the team's success: we all rejoice at each other's achievements and feel sorrow at each other's failures. This sense of closeness satisfies our needs for belonging and gives us the confidence to reach for greater self- realization.

Emotional support of this kind is fundamental to the team's identity. And it can only arise from a set of relationships that seek cooperation rather than competition. Of course, friendly competition within a team is no bad thing: it can help to set new standards and stimulates team members to emulate best practice. But without trust, competition can become damaging. Trust is the final component of these conversations. The clear rule here is: 'assume constructive intent'. Sticking to this rule – particularly when things go wrong – is a valuable first step in putting things right. It ensures that an instant negative reaction is supplanted by a positive attempt to explore what happened, why it happened, and how to stop it happening again.

TEAM MEETINGS

Teams must meet frequently. The danger for any regular meeting is that it can become routine: soon it comes to be regarded more with dread than interest. The solution might be to change the way you run the meetings.

Regular team meetings

A team leader who is willing to delegate functions will lead team meetings that are more active, more interesting and more successful. Consider holding your next team meeting like this:

❑ The team leader constructs the agenda informally prior to the meeting. Anyone who wants to contribute sends a note or adds it to the list. E-mail is particularly valuable for this.

❑ Finalize the agenda at the start of the meeting. Each participant must justify the inclusion of their item. The meeting decides whether it is worthy of discussion (perhaps another team member can solve the problem outside the meeting: a brief conversation, a memo, a report put in the internal post).

❑ All items decided on for the agenda are given timings. The whole meeting has a maximum length – decided on by the team leader – that it must not exceed. The aim is not to fill the allotted time, but to complete the meeting as quickly as possible.

❑ The agenda is now complete. Nothing else is allowed until the next meeting.

❑ Each item is 'owned' by the participant who submitted it. As discussion progresses, they must ask:
  – Is the task or problem clearly understood?
  – Is expertise being identified?
  – Is knowledge being shared?
  – Am I creating a cooperative climate in the group?
  – Is everyone being heard?
  – Can a decision be reached by consensus – without a vote?
  – Is the chair's role reduced to a minimum?

❑ The chair for each item becomes the minute-taker for the next item, recording the minutes on a flip chart for all to see.

❑ Timings are adhered to strictly: they are the responsibility of the team as a whole.

❑ At the end of the meeting, decisions and actions are summarized by the team leader, who then invites any initial suggestions for the next meeting.

This procedure increases the team's ownership of the meeting. A climate of openness allows all views to be expressed with equal authority; solutions are arrived at by agreement rather than imposed. In one company where it was introduced, the time spent in team meetings was cut by a third.

Team briefing and performance review

Team briefing develops the team meeting into a management information system. The objective of team briefing is to ensure that every employee knows and understands what they and others in the organization are doing – and why. Team leaders and their teams get together regularly, for about half an hour, to talk about issues relevant to them and their work. The team leader's brief is based on a 'core brief' supplied by senior management; but, along with this cascade element of information relayed down the line, each team leader writes his or her own brief.

The advocates of team briefing emphasize that it also allows teams to evaluate the brief, assess its relevance to their own work, and communicate in turn back up the line. There are a number of other benefits of team briefing:

❑ **It reinforces management.** The briefing meeting is an opportunity for the team leader to lead. This is particularly important for first-line managers, reminding them of their leadership responsibilities and of their accountability for their team's performance. Team briefing gives management credibility, and ensures that the team hears management information from a manager.

❑ **It increases commitment.** Briefing improves the team's commitment to its objectives, and to those of the organization. Explaining why a job needs doing is as important as telling people that it has to be done.

❑ **It prevents misunderstandings.** The grapevine of rumour and speculation is often a threat to team morale and effectiveness. Team briefing helps to keep the vine well pruned!

❑ **It helps to facilitate change.** As Peter Senge has observed, people do not resist change; they resist being changed. Team briefing helps to keep people in touch with what is happening and gives them the means to contribute to change rather than be victims of it.

❑ **It improves upward communication.** Asking people for ideas in an information vacuum is like asking them to think without brain cells. People will probably not volunteer ideas if they are not asked for them: briefing gives senior management the regular opportunity to make that request. It also provides a permanent channel for feedback and other upward communication.

Team briefing, unlike more informal team meetings, must be led by team leaders. Because the briefer should be the manager accountable for the team's performance, it may make more sense to brief people in work teams rather than according to managerial status: line managers with their production line team, for example, rather than with other managers. The choice of briefer can be affected, too, by the size of teams: if teams are too small or too large, communication, control and interaction all suffer.

The success of team briefing depends on fostering genuine dialogue. There is a danger that team briefing can become merely a system of top-down information flow, conducted in a paternalistic, quasi-military manner. It can be easy for senior management to assume that teams need only to know about decisions to commit to them.

Team briefing must also be systematic to be thoroughly effective. If you are a team leader, you can set up briefings yourself, but they will be much more effective if they are part of a wider communication process and structure within your organization.

Team performance review takes team briefing one step further still. It allows people to see how they are working together by measuring their performance against objectives and targets. As team leader, you can also use the meeting to feed back your impressions of how things are going, and relate the team's work to that of other teams. You can even use it to ask the team how they think you are doing!

Hold team briefings and performance reviews regularly: not just in a crisis, or when things are going badly. Monthly reviews are common. Ensure that the whole team attends (you may wish to hold two meetings if the team is of more than 20 people, if certain operations must be covered constantly or if you operate in shifts). Observe the following guidelines:

❏ Hold the meeting at the beginning of the working day or shift.
❏ Hold it always in paid time.
❏ The meeting should last between 10 and 40 minutes.
❏ Hold the review at the workplace, in a quiet area away from phones and other interruptions.
❏ Create a friendly, positive atmosphere.

Cover the 'Four Ps':

❏ **Progress.** Our achievements. Include individual achievements if appropriate. Reflect back to the team what we have done so far to reach our goals. Start with progress because it helps to create a positive feeling in the team.
❏ **Policy.** How developments elsewhere in the organization are affecting what we are doing.
❏ **People.** Any relevant matters affecting team members that will strengthen the team.
❏ **Points for action.** What we need to do in the future. Any new targets, or special points for action.

As you deliver information from senior management, take care to present it positively, and anticipate any likely questions. Use your language and the team's vocabulary – not that of senior management or 'organizationspeak'. Give concrete examples to support your ideas; answer questions honestly or arrange to answer them later.

Meetings as team laboratories

Meetings are where teams can act most clearly as teams. A meeting is also the place where you can exercise your leadership most openly. It's important, therefore, to manage the team's behaviour at meetings. What's acceptable within the confines of the meeting will be seen by the team as generally acceptable elsewhere.

So think of a meeting as a laboratory in which you are testing and refining the behaviours and values of your team. Broadly, we can categorize team behaviours as:

❑ **task behaviour:** contributions to the team's task objectives;
❑ **process behaviour:** helping the team to develop and strengthen;
❑ **non-functional behaviour:** includes anything that hinders or prevents the team from succeeding in either its task or process objectives.

Task behaviours
These include:

❑ initiating: defining a problem, redefining it, making suggestions, presenting new information, proposing solutions;
❑ seeking information;
❑ giving information;
❑ setting standards;
❑ coordinating: relating ideas to each other, comparing information;
❑ building and elaborating: developing ideas, giving examples, adding detail, creating scenarios;
❑ summarizing: restating, reorganizing information, repeating and clarifying;
❑ evaluating: for value or relevance;

❏ diagnosing: seeking causes of problems;
❏ testing for consensus or disagreement.

Process behaviours
These include:

❏ encouraging: responding positively, praising, accepting;
❏ gatekeeping: letting others contribute;
❏ stopping: ending a line of argument that seems unproductive or counter-intuitive;
❏ following: listening and triggering more from others;
❏ redirecting: from one person to another;
❏ expressing group feeling;
❏ mediating: in moments of conflict;
❏ relieving tension: by suggesting a break or injecting humour.

Non-functional behaviour
Non-functional behaviour makes meetings last too long, stray from the agenda or collapse in confusion. It also provides important clues about strains and unresolved issues in the team. It includes:

❏ aggression;
❏ blocking;
❏ self-confessing or seeking sympathy;
❏ competing;
❏ special pleading;
❏ seeking attention;
❏ negative or offensive humour;
❏ withdrawing.

Distinguishing between these three categories can be difficult, especially if the team includes people of different cultural backgrounds. As team leader, focusing on objectives and targets – as well as on the clock – you will be hard pressed to identify more than a few of these behaviours. You may be reacting to many of them unconsciously.

Separating task direction from process direction can be useful. Using an external facilitator is valuable. However, picking and responding to only a few of these behaviours, then encouraging or discouraging them, can improve the team's performance substantially, both within the meeting and outside.

BUILDING YOUR TEAM

Building a group of people into a team is one of the most satisfying of management tasks. It is also a long-term process. Don't expect extraordinary results in a few days.

Your objective in building a team should be to create a group of people in which:

- ❑ leadership (particularly task leadership) is shared at different times;
- ❑ accountability becomes collective;
- ❑ the team has its own identifiable purpose;
- ❑ problem-solving becomes a way of life;
- ❑ the team's effectiveness is evaluated collectively.

Your responsibilities as a team-builder include:

- ❑ setting and maintaining team objectives;
- ❑ establishing and promoting team values: social, behavioural, task-oriented;
- ❑ maintaining the identity of the team;
- ❑ helping the team always to be outward-looking: welcoming new people and ideas, proactive in the wider organization and with customers or partners;
- ❑ communicating effectively with the team and helping team members communicate with each other;
- ❑ involving the team as much as you can in decisions that relate to them.

Everything about an effective team relies on the team's sense of cohesion. Without trust, respect and openness, nothing else is possible. However creative or adventurous you want the team to become, the basic needs in Maslow's hierarchy – the functional needs of any human being in a group – must be satisfied.

Encouraging cooperation

Cooperation, of course, means operating together. The more people's work is integrated into a single operation, the more they will cooperate.

In practice, cooperation is usually vulnerable to competition. Competition arises out of a natural desire to succeed: if our success depends on denying cooperation to another team member, we will begin to compete. Competition may help individuals achieve, but it will not help a team to develop (though it may help a team win against another team – but that's another story…). Trying to do well and trying to beat someone else are two different things. When they are aligned, competition may have some value. Mostly they are not aligned and the team's performance suffers as a result.

Cooperation helps the team to share resources; it helps the team take advantage of the diverse skills of individuals; and it fosters the social behaviours that we have seen underlie teamwork. The more you can foster cooperation within your team – and between the team and others – the more cohesive and effective your team will become.

Fostering trust

Times are not good for trust. Why should anybody trust senior managements that regularly merge, downsize, lay off and award themselves extravagant bonuses? Your biggest task in building your team may be fostering trust within an organizational culture that doesn't value trust at all.

How can you do it? It's a long-term strategy. Trust needs to be earned; it cannot be demanded. It means treating people as mature adults. It also means engaging in six specific management practices:

❑ **Communicate openly.** Keep the team informed. Explain policy changes and provide accurate feedback on performance. Be candid about your own problems and the limits of your own action responsibility. Tell the truth.

❑ **Support the team.** Be available and approachable. Provide help, advice, coaching and support for team members' ideas.

❑ **Give respect.** Delegation is the most powerful sign of respect you can give. Actively listen to others' ideas and demonstrate that you are thinking, 'What's good about this idea?'

❑ **Be fair.** Give credit where it's due and recognition to those who deserve it. Brush up your appraisal skills.

❑ **Be consistent.** Keep your promises. Practise what you preach. Live the values of your team. Aim to be predictable in your day-to-day dealings with people.

❑ **Lead by example.** Enhance your credibility with your team by demonstrating your competence, your ability, your professionalism and your commitment to the team.

Handling failure

All your leadership skills will come into play when the team faces failure. If goals have not been met, if targets have been missed, if the task or project went wrong or missed its deadline, you have to pull the team together and take it forward.

If the shortcoming is due directly to the people in your team, it may be difficult to handle. But suppose your team – or even the organization as a whole – fails to meet its targets through no fault of its own? Maybe the goals were over-optimistic in the first place. Maybe market forces intervened. Now you face your most challenging leadership task.

❏ You are responsible for keeping the full commitment of your team in tough times. People need encouragement, not punishment. Hardly anything goes according to plan, but the evidence is overwhelming that organizations – and teams – that plan do better than those that don't.

❏ Remind the team of the positive results, and of the positive actions that are being taken to put things right. If the actions are emergency measures, put the message over enthusiastically.

❏ Never avoid responsibility. Never blame others for your team's failure. If you do, you are undermining yourself and your team; your credibility as a leader will come under severe strain.

❏ In dealing with individuals, remember that failure is always depressing. If people can see no prospect of success, they will lose heart. You may need to increase the frequency of your one-to-ones, or walk the job more often, or hold more frequent informal team meetings. You may also need to amend the targets and goals you have set.

❏ After a heavy defeat, the football manager will urge the team to keep their heads up. This is because the manager is already planning for the next game and needs to preserve morale. Don't allow heads to droop. Think of all the positive ways in which you can boost your team's morale.

Teams as complex adaptive systems

Teams as *what*? Complex adaptive systems are composed of elements arranged to form a system that can adapt to its environment. All living creatures are complex adaptive systems, and a lot of thinking is currently exploring the idea that organizations, too, behave rather like organisms in a continually changing environment.

You could think of your team in the same way. It isn't a functional or mechanical unit within a larger mechanism. It is a collection of living and intelligent beings seeking to operate as an effective living system within its environment. That environment is made up of other teams and the rest of the organization. It also includes anyone else the team has contact with, or who affects its operation: customers, suppliers, business partners, management consultants, domestic partners, children, friends... Once you start looking at a team in this way, you begin to see just how complex it is. The complexity derives from its life in its environment. It acts on its environment and is affected by changes in it.

The most effective teams live and work within their environments. A team never exists as a hermetically sealed unit. Its outputs are in the outside world and it must be forever aware of what's going on out there. Indeed, one of the defining features of a complex adaptive system is that the boundary between 'in here' and 'out there' is fuzzy.

An effective team, then, at its very best:

❑ has a special sense of purpose in the world;
❑ retains a unique identity (just as you retain your identity even though your cells replace themselves);
❑ sees current reality as an ally (and isn't constantly fighting against outside influences or blaming failure on external circumstances);
❑ perceives and works with the forces for change;
❑ is deeply inquisitive;
❑ co-evolves with its environment.

As a broad strategy for evolving such a team – and I choose the word to emphasize that teams are living things and not mechanisms that we can engineer – follow some simple principles.

❑ View the team as a community, not as an operational unit. What do communities need? How would you recognize one? What could you do to treat your team as a community? How could the team start to behave more like a community?
❑ De-emphasize operational rules. Challenge 'the way it's always been done'. Take your team on regular excursions out of operational thinking and ask: 'What if?'

❑ Invest in multiple interpretations of reality. In other words, value lots of different points of view. Actively encourage people to come up with alternatives to ideas. Invite guests from outside the team. Send the team out to see how things happen elsewhere: in different parts of the organization, on different sites, in different sectors, in other professions. Go to art galleries and concerts.

❑ Practise dialogue. Open up your conversation styles and do everything you can to make them rich exchanges of ideas.

❑ Make information accessible. Make sure that your team knows where to find the knowledge it needs. Encourage people always to find out more. Use databases and libraries. Send people to conferences and seminars outside the organization. Be hungry for new ideas.

7

MANAGING PROJECTS

Sooner or later, you will probably have to manage a project. More and more organizations see projects as the main means of delivering real change, if not the only one.

Project management cuts across all the normal functional responsibilities of a manager. It requires special skills of you as a leader, as a planner and organizer, and as a motivator. All the skills we have explored in this book will be useful to you as a project manager. The way you exercise them in this context, however, will be different.

The word 'project' often comes with certain preconceptions attached. You probably think of projects as being:

❑ extremely technical;
❑ complicated;
❑ full of jargon;
❑ burdened with lots of paperwork.

Some projects are all four! But, equally, many simpler tasks are called projects. Excessive documentation remains a problem for many project managers, although some organizations now encourage managers to use software to create and manage project records.

In this chapter, we will explore the essentials of managing projects. Project managers need to manage people in very specific ways, and it is these new people skills that we concentrate on here.

WHAT IS A PROJECT?

A project is simply a special task. To develop the definition a little, we can say that a project is a piece of work with defined objectives and a single defined outcome. Projects exist to create something new. Once that new creation has come into existence, the project is over.

To achieve this single, definable outcome, a project has defined timescales and costs. It usually includes a number of milestones: these, by definition, are stages on the route to success. Each milestone includes a 'deliverable': there is some demonstrable outcome that shows the milestone has been reached. The project team must reach each of these milestones in turn if the end result is to be achieved. Milestones also help the project leader and senior managers to monitor the progress of the project.

Projects exist outside the normal operations of the organization. Operational work is regular, repeated activity that is familiar to those who do it. We do operational work by using existing skills and experience to follow standard procedures and routines. Generally, operational work is predetermined by the needs of the organization through the functional line structure.

Operational work usually has procedures for tackling unexpected situations. Of course, such emergency procedures can only cope with the unexpected situations that the organization has taught itself to expect! When the problem is truly unprecedented, and cannot be resolved with established methods and practices, the organization is faced with the need to change.

Achieving change means working *outside* the boundaries of operational work. New methods, tools and techniques are required and additional skills and capabilities are needed to apply them. Time and cost are given a high profile and attempts are made to define the desired outcome from the work. So everything that happens during the execution of the special task is regarded as part of a temporary group of activities, unique to the task and set apart from operations. The special task has been born as a project.

CHARACTERISTICS OF A PROJECT

A project differs from operational work in that it:

❑ has a specific purpose;
❑ is usually not routine;
❑ comprises interdependent activities;
❑ has defined time constraints;
❑ is often complex;
❑ has defined cost constraints;
❑ is subject to cancellation;
❑ must be flexible and responsive to change;
❑ involves many unknowns;
❑ involves risk.

A project has a life of its own. Indeed, it has a limited life cycle, involving conception, birth, growth, achievement and death. It will almost certainly have to evolve, change shape or direction and respond to organizational needs as they change. (So a project, like a team, is a complex adaptive system.) But it must retain its identity if it is to survive. A project's identity is defined by its objectives. Everybody involved in the project must give mutual effort in a controlled way to achieve their objectives.

The tools, techniques and methods employed to manage all projects are broadly similar. They differ only according to the length and complexity of the project. Managers usually select complex analytical planning and monitoring tools only for large and costly projects. On short projects involving only a few people, simpler methods and procedures will normally suffice. The essential *skills* of managing a project, though, are the same no matter how large or small the project.

Difficulties with projects

The nature of projects and their fundamental characteristics as non-operational work create a host of potential difficulties. Here is a (depressingly long) list of some pitfalls that lie in wait for you as a project manager:

- ❑ no time for effective planning;
- ❑ unclear authority and accountability;
- ❑ unrealistic timescales;
- ❑ lack of appreciation of the amount of work involved;
- ❑ lack of real time and personal 'overload';
- ❑ poor estimating of time needed;
- ❑ functional barriers and poor cooperation;
- ❑ empire-building;
- ❑ poor morale ('Why are we doing this?');
- ❑ low motivation;
- ❑ personality clashes;
- ❑ the wrong team membership;
- ❑ conflict in management team;
- ❑ nobody 'owns' the project;
- ❑ interference by 'outsiders';
- ❑ everyone else is responsible (the 'Don't Blame Me' syndrome);
- ❑ no consistent approach ('We don't do things that way round here').

Dealing with, or avoiding, these problems involves understanding the full scope of the project, the structure of responsibility by which you will lead it, and the stages of the life cycle that your project will follow.

THE PROJECT WINDOW

Take a look out of the window. If you are unfortunate enough to have an office without a window, take a look through your manager's office window!

What do you see? If you are some distance from the window, your view will be limited. Objects closer to you will occupy your attention and interfere with the information you receive from outside. If you move closer to the window, the view changes. You probably won't be able to take in everything at once: you must scan right and left, up and down, to take it all in. Repeated scans may be necessary to gather all the information. Your interest and curiosity lead you even closer to the window to see everything. You have become involved with all the information presented through the window, shutting out local distractions.

The same circumstances apply to leading a project. When you are appointed as the leader, the project window makes its first appearance. At this point, the window probably looks small because it is distant, and is likely to have the following characteristics:

❑ The project data available are limited, often just a general description or 'terms of reference' which may be supported by a feasibility study carried out much earlier.
❑ The project specification is probably vague. Little planning has been carried out, and nobody has any real idea what is involved.
❑ The project will certainly have some objectives, although these are not always immediately obvious to you. The stated objectives are often unclear and sometimes even misguided.
❑ Availability of resources has probably received little attention, but somebody may have set a budget limit.

So your view through the window is very limited. The information available to you is constrained by the views of those who first thought up the project. You will have many distractions at this point, principally day-to-day operational activities. These have to continue and your project role is an additional burden, which can lead to additional stress.

If the project is to start well, you have to move quickly closer to the window. The view is confusing and hazy. You must consider the resources available and start to assemble the core team for the project. This may comprise people from your own team or close associates. The next major leap forward is the key to the success of the whole project. It is made up of two giant steps:

❑ putting the project in context;
❑ identifying all those with an interest in the project.

The window currently gives little or no information on either and you cannot start the planning process without these inputs to enlarge the view.

Putting the project in context

Both you and the core team need to understand the context of the project in the organization. You need answers to questions such as:

❑ How does this fit into corporate strategy?
❑ Why is it necessary?
❑ What has been done before?
❑ What is the real purpose of the project?
❑ Why are we selected for the project?
❑ What will we gain from the project if it succeeds?
❑ What happens if we fail?
❑ What will the organization gain from the project?
❑ What are the expectations of the senior management?

Getting answers to these and other questions creates a vision for the project and removes some of the haze in the project window. The core team will become more involved with the project. They will understand the reasons behind it and the risks involved in tackling it.

Identifying the stakeholders

The stakeholders include anybody who has an interest in the project's outcome. This starts with you and the core team: your interest is obvious. But there will always be many others with a vested interest in all or parts of the project life cycle as well as its results.

Every project should have a sponsor, a senior manager who is directly sponsoring the project and is accountable at senior level. Identify this sponsor and get to know them quickly. With the help of your team, you must then assess all the other possible stakeholders. All of them will have different perceptions of the project's purpose and expectations of its outcome. All have a contribution to make. In addition, each stakeholder will bring their own agenda, values, styles and aspirations that they will apply to the project.

The stakeholders fall into two groups:

❑ internal;
❑ external.

You must first secure the support and commitment of the internal stakeholders. Politics will always influence the degree of cooperation you will be able to achieve across functional boundaries. Your project has to compete for resources with other projects, as well as with day-to-day operations. Other managers may believe they should lead your project because they believe they could do a better job. This element of competition and resentment may create difficult relationships and conflict.

The external stakeholders may include the end user *and* the client (who may not be the same), the local community, external institutions, suppliers, consultants and contractors. Their influence may be central or on the fringes, either at the start or much later in the project life cycle.

Managing all of these stakeholders may be the most difficult managerial challenge you will face in running a project. You have limited authority over most of them and you may find it difficult to influence them to your advantage. Nonetheless, you must find a way to manage them effectively so that they remain positive in supporting you and your project.

PROJECT LEADERSHIP

Project leadership sits outside the range of your responsibilities as a functional manager. A project is inherently beyond the normally accepted line hierarchy of the organization. It will establish unusual and short-term links to managers at all levels. It may not always be clear how you should make and maintain these links. Lines of responsibility and accountability may be ill defined and few established practices may exist. You find yourself in an unusual position: outside the normal hierarchy, with freedom to determine your own rules, but also vulnerable to opposition from colleagues, subordinates and senior managers. Project leaders are often perceived, perhaps inevitably, as interfering with the smooth running of the business.

Well – that's as it should be. If you are not delivering change through your project, why are you devoting so much energy to it? How does your project align to the wider objectives of the organization? Who is your sponsor? What weight can they lend to your project? Above all, why do *you* believe in this project? Without your strong commitment to change and to achieving your objectives, your project – like so many others – may be doomed to fail.

Key characteristics of a project leader

The project leader is:

❑ responsible for achieving the project objectives;
❑ clearly in charge of the project and hence in a position of high risk;

❏ limited in authority to get resources inside and outside the organization;
❏ expected to get results, cutting across established procedures and customs;
❏ expected to operate in unknown and unpredictable areas to achieve results;
❏ susceptible to low credibility with other managers and regarded with suspicion.

Project leadership has three essential dimensions:

❏ identifying and managing the stakeholders;
❏ managing the project life cycle;
❏ managing the team's performance (and the performance of everybody else involved).

So project management is a more complex role than line management. The first two of these dimensions have little or no influence on the line manager's normal daily operating activities. For a project leader, in contrast, they have a high profile.

Project management can seem to require you to be superhuman. You must identify the skills necessary for the project at any particular time, and ensure that they are used effectively, in accordance with your plans and schedules. You have to orchestrate the work across numerous interdepartmental interfaces: you must open doors and break down walls. Success lies in your ability to control the project process; to know what is happening when and where, and to take appropriate action when problems appear.

A model for project leadership

Action-centred leadership provides the basic model. In project management, however, your control as leader must extend the model in two directions:

❏ **Inner-directed leadership.** The three areas of concern – achieving the task, developing individuals and building the team – are now centred around one specific outcome: the project.

The project leader is in a position to ensure that the project objectives are kept in high profile at all times and to keep the project process going in the right direction.

In this process you are constantly monitoring that:
– scheduled work is carried out;
– deadlines are met on time;
– the team is working well together;
– all individuals are equipped with the skills needed.

You are always moving between the three functional areas: coordinating the work, making sure the team has sufficient resources and is clear about its purpose and responsibilities, and helping any individual who needs it. Throughout these activities you are concerned to stand back and take an overview from the centre, to see that everything is going to plan.

If you are confined to these areas of activity, the project process is likely to be effectively under control. But you are operating in a confined situation – the inner workings of the project process.

❏ **Outer-directed leadership.** Your management skills need to extend beyond the team to the stakeholders. You must act as an interface between the project and the wider environment of the organization.

These stakeholders are on the outer fringes of the project process and most are probably not involved in the activities of the project team. Yet they can influence the project directly and indirectly and must be brought into your sphere of operating control.

So you must expand your sphere of influence. All the stakeholders must be brought into the operating area and your efforts must also become *outer-directed.*

As the project leader, you have the holistic role of managing and controlling the project process, the team, the team members and all the stakeholders to achieve the objectives. You must continually look inwards and outwards. You must lead the team and act as the project's ambassador in the wider circle of stakeholders.

Project leadership begins to look rather like a combination of orchestral conductor and seasoned diplomat. You will need excellent influencing and negotiating skills to keep all the elements in balance.

THE PROJECT LIFE CYCLE

At every stage of the project you will follow a process that has five basic steps. This process is applicable to the project as a whole, and is equally applicable to any individual part of the project plan.

Step one: defining objectives and deadlines

You need to define the overall project and task objectives, at the same time making sure that the team understands these in context. You must scope the project: set its limits and the areas you will influence. You must take particular care at this point to ensure that everyone can accept their involvement in the work ahead. All objectives should have clear deadlines, clearly identified results and defined benefits. It is essential at this stage that you demonstrate your own commitment and enthusiasm for the project.

Step two: preparing the plan and schedules

With clear objectives established, the planning process usually follows two stages:

❏ fact-finding;
❏ decision-taking.

The team must be involved in both stages if you are to continue building their commitment to the project.

❏ Fact-finding is an information-gathering process to ensure that all relevant data are collected together for the planning process. You encourage ideas and suggestions and consult team members, colleagues and others to generate all available relevant data on any particular aspect of the project. This will comprise a mixture of historical experience, facts, opinions and legend. All will have to be sorted and filtered to provide really useful information.
❏ Decision-taking is the process of drawing conclusions for action from the alternatives and options generated during fact-finding. You will present this information in different ways, according to who needs it and how it is to be used. It's prudent to keep some options for action available as contingencies if a plan fails to work out.

Step three: briefing the team and stakeholders

Having identified all the activities of the plan, you must tell everybody involved:

❏ what has to be done;
❏ when things are to be done;
❏ the deadlines.

This stage is vital to generating 'ownership' in the team and the stakeholders. You need to know that each individual clearly understands their action responsibilities. Of course, it is not practical to give all the detail at the start-up. Some details will not even be available: many of the work plans will only be developed as the project proceeds. Nevertheless, each team member must clearly understand their role and how they should interact with other team members and stakeholders.

Step four: monitoring progress and support

You have established the climate and environment for the work to proceed. You must now ensure motivation is maintained at a high level, dealing promptly with problems as they arise. These may be technical, administrative or resource problems. You will need to look inwards and outwards a good deal.

Walking the job is vital to find out what is going on and how you can help. This visible leadership is essential to encourage the team and show an interest in their welfare and progress.

Step five: evaluating results

Evaluation doesn't happen only at the end of the project. You must also evaluate as the project proceeds. Through regular contact with the team and the stakeholders, you can determine if the project is on track, and that its results are meeting expectations. You can identify whether your planning has been effective, correct and comprehensive. This will allow you to work out whether a change of direction is needed, and take steps to modify your plans.

When the project finally ends, carry out a full post-project evaluation. Identify the key learning points of the project and record these for future reference.

These five steps can be regarded as a cyclic process. In practice, the action cycle is a multitude of cycles, each at different stages of progress. Blockages can appear at any time. New information may become available, fact-finding may have been inadequate or communications may have suffered within the team and between the team and the stakeholders. You may find the objectives revised as one or more stakeholders 'move the goalposts' without informing you in good time. Your plans may show shortcomings as the team comes up with better ideas and you must decide whether to modify the schedules. In fact, at any stage of any cycle, the processes may need repeating to resolve problems and derive ways to bypass the blockages. This is a dynamic process, which enables you to maintain control and keep the project moving. These five steps are the key result areas where you take action as project leader to achieve ultimate success.

THE PROJECT TEAM

As the project leader you are working to get results with and through the project team. You must energize and direct this diverse group to give high performance, willingly, throughout the project life.

You must lead the project team, often with minimal legitimate line authority over their actions. In many organizations, different departments have their own departmental culture. Inter-departmental barriers can arise as departments protect their interests. You have to overcome these barriers and create a climate of cooperation.

Most project teams are multifunctional. You must weld into a single team a group of people from different areas, with different needs, backgrounds, experience and skills. Many of these team members will only be giving part of their working day or week to the project. Success in project management depends critically on your ability to build this effective team rapidly and maintain its performance.

QUALITIES OF A SUCCESSFUL PROJECT TEAM

The most important qualities are:

❑ commitment to the project;
❑ result-oriented attitude;
❑ innovative and creative thinking;
❑ willingness to change;
❑ concern for quality;
❑ ability to predict trends;
❑ high involvement, interest and energy;
❑ capacity to quickly resolve conflict;
❑ good communications and feedback;
❑ mutual trust and confidence;
❑ interest in self-development;
❑ effective organizational interfacing.

You most certainly won't create a successful project team without clear leadership. You must understand the barriers and difficulties that your team has to overcome. These might include:

❑ unclear initial project objectives;
❑ inadequate resources;
❑ power games and conflict;
❑ lack of support and commitment of senior management;
❑ poor job security;
❑ moving goals, objectives and priorities.

Taking action to avoid these problems is an essential activity for a project leader. Principally, this means understanding and operating the whole project management process – and anticipating problems before they happen!

Building the project team

Clearly, there are many problems to be faced by the project leader forming a new project team. Many are normal and predictable but still interfere with team-building and performance. Typically, such areas to pay particular attention to are:

❑ confusion of roles;
❑ unclear responsibilities;
❑ unclear channels of authority;
❑ uneven work distribution;
❑ assignments unclear;
❑ overall objectives unclear;
❑ stakeholders not identified or managed;
❑ mistrust in leader and other team members;
❑ individual objectives unrelated to project;
❑ commitment to project plan lacking;
❑ poor team spirit;
❑ suspicion;
❑ lack of leadership;
❑ conflict and personality clashes.

A successful project team never simply happens. It must be worked for. You will earn the team's trust by developing the team's identity and looking after the interests of its members. You will earn their respect by focussing on the work. The project is not the most important thing, but it does come first. This means sometimes making unpopular decisions in the interest of the project. Keep people focused on the project, and on its deadline, and they will be much more likely to work with you.

MOTIVATING YOUR PROJECT TEAM

Here are some guidelines for success:

❑ Involve all the team in the planning process.
❑ Ensure they all understand their action responsibilities in the project.
❑ Learn about team members' skills, experience, expectations and needs.
❑ Involve them in problem-solving and seek their ideas and suggestions.
❑ Keep everyone well informed of progress, including all stakeholders.
❑ Help team members to schedule and prioritize their work-load when necessary.
❑ Establish a decision-taking process and seek consensus from the team.
❑ Review performance regularly through one-to-one meet-ings and set targets.
❑ Establish a motivating climate and hold regular short team meetings.
❑ Resolve conflicts and grievances promptly.
❑ Celebrate success and learn from the failures.

AND FINALLY...

Many managers are expected to take responsibility for projects with little or no additional specialist training or understanding of the skills required. This short-sighted approach can lead to disaster. Project management should be included as a core managerial competency. If you feel that your level of skills for the job is not adequate to give you a strong sense of self-confidence, seek additional training now.

APPENDIX

WHERE TO GO FROM HERE

Managing people is a continuous journey of discovery. Becoming more skilled in conversation, in balancing the complex needs of other people, the task, and your organization is a never-ending learning process. Here are some suggestions for pursuing the ideas that we've already explored.

CHAPTER 1: MANAGEMENT BY CONVERSATION

The idea of management as a continuing conversation is at the heart of Michael Wallacek's work with The Industrial Society. His programme, *Klausur*, is an intensive exploration of management by conversation.

The Industrial Society also runs a large number of courses in all the areas covered in this book. Contact them by phone on 0171 479 1000 or visit their website: www.indsoc.co.uk

For more on skilful conversation, see Peter Senge's *The Fifth Discipline* (Century, London, 1990) and *The Fifth Discipline Workbook* (Nicholas Brealey, London, 1994). Bill Isaacs has developed an impressive body of ideas on dialogue. Find him by visiting the MIT website (*web.mit.edu*) and searching for 'Bill Isaacs'.

CHAPTER 2: MODELS OF PEOPLE MANAGEMENT

All the models in this chapter are well known and referred to in many standard texts on management. A particularly strong and comprehensive overview is *Organizational Behaviour* by Kreitner, Kinicki and Buelens (McGraw-Hill, Maidenhead, 1999).

For more on Action-centred Leadership, see John Adair's *The Action-centred Leader* (The Industrial Society, London, 1988). Look also at the society's leadership courses, particularly their Runge Balliol programme.

To find out more on memes and other ideas from the new science that are impinging on management, look at *Navigating Complexity* by Arthur Battram (The Industrial Society, London, 1998).

CHAPTER 3: MANAGING YOURSELF

Andrew Forrest summarizes the five dimensions of management in *5 Way Management* (The Industrial Society, London, 1997). On stress and time management, see the excellent *The Stress Workbook* by Eve Warren and Caroline Toll (Nicholas Brealey, London, 1996).

CHAPTER 4: MANAGING THE WORK

On the elements of performance management, take a look at Roger Moores's *Managing for High Performance* (The Industrial Society, London, 1994).

Jane Weightman's *Competencies in Action* (Institute of Personnel and Development, London, 1994) is a good place to continue looking at this rather specialized area of people management.

CHAPTER 5: DEVELOPING PEOPLE

As well as Peter Senge's work (already mentioned), Tony Atherton's *How to Be Better at Delegation and Coaching* (Kogan Page, London, 1999) is particularly strong on these areas.

CHAPTER 6: MANAGING A TEAM

For more on teams, look at Rupert Eales-White's *How to Be a Better Teambuilder* (Kogan Page, London, 1996).

CHAPTER 7: MANAGING PROJECTS

The literature on project management grows vaster every day. A good starting place is the work of Trevor Young: his three books, *Planning Projects*, *Implementing Projects* and *Leading Projects* (all published by The Industrial Society, London, 1993) form an excellent detailed introduction to this increasingly important style of management.

Project management is also particularly well served by internet resources. Go to www.projectnet.co.uk as a good starting-point.

INDEX

Visit Kogan Page on-line

Comprehensive information on
Kogan Page titles

Features include

- complete catalogue listings,
  including book reviews and
  descriptions

- on-line discounts on a variety
  of titles

- special monthly promotions

- information and discounts on
  NEW titles and BESTSELLING titles

- a secure shopping basket facility
  for on-line ordering

- infoZones, with links and
  information on specific areas of
  interest

PLUS everything you need to know
about KOGAN PAGE

http://www.kogan-page.co.uk